Advance Praise for
Anti-Aging God's Way

Bobbie Gee has been an inspiration to me since the day I met her and gives all that she has so that others can achieve all that they can. I was blessed to have heard her life-changing message, which taught me that I owe it to myself to believe that I can truly accomplish anything. Bobbie is a mentor who truly cares about each person in her sphere of influence. As a caring mother, grandmother, and wife, she has built a home that is an oasis of love and comfort for those who enter it.

—SHERI BARRY
Certified Image Consultant and Business Owner

Something was missing. I then took Bobbie Gee's class, "It's About You." The impact on my life was immediate. I became more self-aware and was able to ask important questions about self-image, character, and confidence. I learned to think about who I am and what I was offering to the people in my life. Bobbie taught me to become comfortable with the uncomfortable and forced me to confront my own character. She said, "Character is your ability to carry out a resolution long after the mood in which it was made has passed." And my confidence grew as I did what I feared doing and stopped comparing myself with others. Now my stagnant business is thriving, and I am able to transfer what I learned from Bobbie to others. I feel good about making a difference in other people's lives.

—DIANE WITTE
Executive Sales, Sensaria Natural Bodycare

I had a successful career and a happy marriage. But my soul ached for more and through Bobbie Gee's workshop, I discovered a relationship with God. My life now reflects the grace that I have found, and I can share it with others. Now I know that my body is God's temple, and I keep it fit and healthy. Even my skin glows, as I rest in God's peace.

—CHRISTINE KELTON
Attorney and Professor of Law

While attending Bobbie Gee's workshop, I discovered my own core beliefs. In this process of discovery, my attitudes toward myself and life began to change, as did those of two close friends. We all three found love and are so thankful for Bobbie's life-changing help.

—TERRIE PETERSEN BATTLE
Executive Assistant, Mecca Artist Management

Anti-Aging
God's Way

A Fascinating First Look
at Anti-Aging
from a Spiritual Perspective

BOBBIE GEE

sei
publishing

A division of Sound Enterprises, Inc.

Published by SEI Publishing, an imprint of Sound Enterprises, Inc., Spokane, Washington (www.SEIzoom.com).

First Printing—September 2010

ISBN-13: 978-1-935811-02-2

Printed in the United States of America

To Ernie,

For all the kindness, gentleness, and patience
you have given me throughout our many years together.
The power of your love changed my life.
Your love fills my empty spaces.
You are truly unforgettable.

Acknowledgments

First, I must acknowledge the impact my mother had on my life. Her example of inward and outward beauty, as well as her faith in God, gave me a fabulous foundation to build on.

To my remarkable husband, Ernie, who has always encouraged, nurtured, and believed in me. I thank him for the countless hours on the computer. Without him interpreting my dyslexia in spelling and sentence structure, I am quite sure this book would have never been published.

A big thank you to Shien-Lin Garrett, for her generosity of her time to contribute her medical expertise to this book. With a full patient load plus four young children, she set time aside to help me with this project.

To Sally Fenton, a precious friend who, after reading the first draft, took it on herself to organize my thoughts and loves me enough to be completely honest with me.

To Joe Lee, Paul Eshleman, and Joanne Wallace, who all read my rough drafts and made suggestions on the book's contents.

To Angel, Rodney, and all the SEI associates. Your belief in the project is an answer to prayer.

To God, for filling my life with such wonderful friends.

Preface

Just as the final rewrite of *Anti-Aging God's Way* was completed, God put me through a test I never expected.

An extended family member, someone I deeply loved, believed in, and had the upmost respect for, hurt me so deeply it went to the very core of my soul. Never in my long and happy life had I felt so betrayed and felt so much pain.

Like everyone, I have experienced sorrow. Once, after twenty years' investment of time and money, a company I founded was stolen from me. The product was produced to save lives and it received the highest rating compared with similar products in *Consumers Report*. After a week of tears, I let it go, knowing the man who did this will one day stand before the Lord and answer for his greed.

That loss was very painful, but it did not come close to the grief caused by the family member I trusted and loved. I said to God, "Lord, I do not understand why this happened to me."

God's answer? "Bobbie, you have enjoyed a wonderful life with little emotional pain. Now, for the first time, you can sincerely, and with full knowledge, relate to many of the women who will read this book or hear you speak. You will know the pain of women who have lost a child, or been deceived by their husband or best friend, or have a serious illness.

"Bobbie, do you sincerely believe what you have written? Will you continue to trust me and practice your beliefs in emotional health and its connection to anti-aging, and know that I am here to carry your burdens?"

I now understand, Lord, that through this betrayal, you allowed me to gain knowledge and wisdom, and gave me insight into the feelings, sadness, and anguish so many people have endured.

Thank you for the experiences—I now have a deeper understanding and a more compassionate heart.

"Life is a succession of lessons
which must be lived to be understood."
(Ralph Waldo Emerson, 1803–1882)

Mother's Wisdom

When I was a young teenager,
my mother sat me down for *the talk*.

The talk covered lifetime skin care, beauty, sun damage, smoking, morals,
integrity, honesty, and any and all guilt-causing transgressions.

A talk that could have lasted hours was over in 30 seconds.

"At 17, you will have the face God gave you.
At 45, you will have the face you deserve."

Enough said!

Contents

Acknowledgments   vii

Preface   ix

Introduction   xvii

PART ONE: THE NON-SURGICAL FACE-LIFT

Looking for the Fountain of Youth   3

Eighty Years of Inspiration   7

The Gift of Health   9

Time-Tested Beauty   11

PART TWO: IT ALL BEGINS WITH A STRONG FOUNDATION

Stone One: How Strong Is Your Foundation?   15

Stone Two: Rock-Solid Standards   17

Stone Three: Future Fundamentals   18

Success God's Way   22

The Ultimate Goal List   23

For Excitement—Take Risks   24

The Final Stone: Your Personal Philosophy   26

PART THREE: THE FIRST STEPS TO ANTI-AGING SUCCESS

The Fruits of a Positive Attitude   31

The Essence of Beauty Is Happiness   35

The Two Most Powerful Forces on Earth:
   the Human Brain and the Human Heart   41

Stressed Out Does Not Make a Beauty Queen   44

Leaving Your Worries on God's Doorstep   53

The Liability of Guilt and the Healing Beauty of Forgiveness   56

The Dangers of Denial   63

Guidelines for Good Decision Making   66

You—Wonderful beyond Imagination   67

The Truth About Self-Worth   69

Authentic Love   77

Contents

PART 4: ANTI-AGING BEAUTY SECRETS

Air and Water—Your Anti-Aging Quick Start 91

From Rock 'n' Roll to Nip and Tuck! 92

Sleeping Beauty 98

The Secrets of Beautiful Skin 103

Olive Oil—Inside and Outside 106

My Private Sanctuary 111

Just Like American Express—Don't Leave Home Without It 114

A Quick Review 115

Preventing Osteoporosis—Through Food and Exercise 118

Common Sense Anti-Aging Tips 121

Let's Talk Food 123

Antioxidants: God's Diet for Anti-Aging and Health 125

Food of the Gods 127

Nature's Nectar 128

Worthy of Thought 130

Words of Inspiration 133

PART 5: COSMETIC PROCEDURES

A Quick Word About Cosmetic Procedures 137

Topicals 139
- Vitamin A • AHAs • Peptides • Antioxidants
- Moisturizers • Injections • Botox • Dysport

Fillers 143
- Collagen • Prevelle Silk • Hylaform • Captique
- Restylane • Perlane • Juvederm Ultra and Juvederm Ultra plus

Fat Transfers 146
- Radiesse • Sculptra (New-Fill)
- Artefill • Silicone

Laser Skin-Tightening Systems 149
- Titan Skin-Tightening • Polaris Skin-Tightening
- Refirme Skin-Tightening • Aluma Skin-Tightening
- LuxIR Skin-Tightening

Dermatological Procedures 152
- Thermage • IPL (Intense Pulsed Light) / Fotofacial
- Levulan Photodynamic Therapy • Chemical Peels • Plasma Resurfacing

Contents

- Lasers   • Laser Skin-Resurfacing   • Facial Laser Resurfacing
- Fractional Laser Resurfacing   • Contour Lift, Feather Lift (APTOS Thread Lift)
- Hair Removal   • Dermabrasion

Surgical Cosmetic Procedures   159
- The Lifestyle Lift   • Mini Face-Lift   • Face-Lift
- Liposuction and Tumescent Liposuction
- What Is Safe for Skin of Color?

PART 6: ANTI-AGING FOR SKIN BY LOCATION AND COMPLAINT

What You Can Do About . . .   163

About the Author   169

Bobbie Gee Enterprises   171

Introduction

The ideas herein represent the knowledge I have gained in my lifetime about anti-aging. I share my beliefs on the effects of aging and its relationship to your emotional well-being, as well as my day-to-day procedures.

I believe we all need a powerful and positive place to leave the toxic feelings and emotions that often destroy a once beautiful and youthful face.

I do not apologize for my references to God throughout this book. My faith in God has had a profound effect on my life, spirit, and happiness, and, I am convinced, on my lack of wrinkles.

My career in the world of skin care and beauty began at age 14. It is now my opinion and accumulated knowledge that successful anti-aging is 25 percent external and 75 percent internal, or "mind over matter." I also believe in the miracle-working power of forgiveness. Emotional health is as important as physical health when they relate to anti-aging.

Emotions such as guilt, resentment, jealousy, and bitterness, just to name a few, must be replaced with acceptance, contentment, peace, and faith. Guilt tortures our souls as happiness refreshes our souls, and every emotion we feel presents itself on our face.

I am a 100 percent believer in the connection of mind, body, and soul. Therefore I have outlined a strong foundation for life and a list of things you can do to achieve positive decision making and avoid the dangers of denial.

I believe my ongoing spiritual growth has been as important as my dedication to skin care through the years. I am thrilled to have the opportunity to share with you my ideas on inner and outer beauty.

You will learn the truth about self-worth, the fruits of a positive attitude, and the wonders of olive oil. You will receive beauty secrets plus a dictionary of cosmetic procedures for your education.

I'm not about to say I know everything there is to know about anti-aging, but I share with you my convictions, things I have learned, things I know work, and things I believe, based on my years in the personal appearance and image business. We all care how we look. The more attractive and youthful we appear, the more opportunities we have in this age-biased society.

We are role models for our children, grandchildren, and great-grandchildren. No matter our age, it is never too late to be an example of femininity, dignity, grace, and style. There is beauty in every woman; we are all connected through our reproductive organs, and hormones, that flow through our bodies. Enjoy your journey down the anti-aging road.

Part One

THE NON-SURGICAL
FACE-LIFT

Looking for the Fountain of Youth

If a fountain of youth were discovered, it would begin with a mind, heart, and soul transformation.

Sigmund Freud (1856–1939) confessed that his "thirty years of research into the feminine soul" left him unable to answer one great question: "What does a woman want?"

I know one answer to that question. Women want to look as good and youthful as possible. We are looking for our own fountain of youth. Every time a new product hits the shelves promising to be the latest miracle anti-aging cream, it flies off the shelves until proven ineffective.

When we meet a woman who appears to have discovered the fountain of youth, most are curious to know her secrets: What products does she use? How does she care for her skin? Is she the product of facial reconstruction or is she just lucky?

Unfortunately, there is no fountain of youth. In the last few years alone, people spent $50 million on one product—DHEA (De-hydroepiandrosterone, a human growth hormone). DHEA promised us the fountain of youth. It now appears after years of study the fountain was full of baloney, according to the New England Journal of Medicine. If you are looking to combat the effects of age on your face, look deep inside your soul. Your spiritual and emotional health are as important to anti-aging as is your devotion to skin care, but most people are still looking for that magic pill to keep those 60 trillion body cells young.

Anti-aging for the pathologically self-obsessed is one-dimensional—plastic surgery. *Anti-Aging God's Way* is three-dimensional—body, mind, and soul. When all three are addressed, you get more than a face-lift; you get a heart-, mind-, and soul-lift. This is a recipe for success. A three-dimensional lift floods every organ of your body with peace, happiness, and joy.

Anti-aging is more than skin deep—it must reach to the heart. The non-surgical face-lift involves happiness, love, forgiveness, and caring. Anti-aging is more than a peel, a lift, Botox, or any cosmetic makeover. Anyone can paint a house, but if there are termites in the house, it is being destroyed from the inside out, and eventually, the house will come tumbling down. The same is true for one's face—a person must be healthy on the inside as well as on the outside.

We have heard it said we are born into this world without a book of instructions, but this is inaccurate. The Bible has been around for generations. If taken seriously and followed, you will find some of the best anti-aging advice ever compiled. It holds information on your emotional health, your physical health, your relationships, your happiness, your parenting skills, and your life-style as a whole. One of my anti-aging secrets is the privilege of having been born into a Christian home where I was introduced to life's true Master of success. I was taught the lifestyle principles of the Bible. When you couple spirituality with common sense and add today's medical advances, you can create a multitude of anti-aging successes, as well as save money by understanding basic anti-aging principles.

I began my career in the field of fashion at the age of 14. I guess you could say I was fortunate to have reached the height of six feet by the tender age of 12. People were so shocked when they met me all they could say was "You should be a model." So at age 14, I was introduced to a teenage modeling agency. What a gift that was to a 124-pound girl who stood a head above the crowd.

God was definitely in charge. After winning a modeling contest at age 16, something very strange happened to me. My high school gym teachers read about the contest in the *Los Angeles Times* and asked me to teach fashion and poise to all the girls' gym classes once a week. When I accepted the challenge without knowing what I was doing, my serious education and mastering the concepts of lasting beauty, skin care, fashion, and self-confidence began. I went to the library and checked out as many books as I could find on the subjects, read like crazy, and taught my classes.

From that day to this, I have continued to study, grow, and educate myself on the mind, body, and soul connection. I now know and have seen demonstrated the results of interaction between the conscious and subconscious minds. For those who think young at 90 and those who think old at 60, these thoughts are interpreted by the muscles of the face. Genes play a large role in an individual's aging/anti-aging profile, but one's own thoughts play an equally powerful role. Negative emotions are powerful enough to destroy your face and health. The negative ideas we entertain defeat our youthfulness. I dislike being around people who constantly talk about how old they feel, and the health issues they face.

The mind-body connection is copiously powerful! Many unforeseen factors can hasten the aging process: death of a loved one, loss of our financial resources, divorce, teenagers, loss of a job we love, marital discord, unhappiness, smoking, infertility, a broken friendship, slander, a serious illness or an unfortunate accident. And did I mention raising teenagers?

At one point in my career, everything I had dreamed of and prayed for was coming true. In my 40s, I was still young, still thin, and probably a little too sure of myself. We must never allow self-confidence to turn into arrogance.

God in his infinite wisdom has his ways to keep us humble. For me, it was called *menopause*. How things changed after the "big M-word!" It appears to me every ounce of food that passes my lips sticks right to my hips.

Since 75 percent of anti-aging success is derived from internal influences, few forces age us more quickly than ill health. Therefore, you must be deliberate in your attempt to stay healthy. Every day, new anti-aging information comes to light on what to eat for better skin and health, anti-oxidants, and wonder drugs. We are told about habits we should form and habits we should break. It gets so confusing, with few proven formulas, some people just give up.

Today's culture implies that wrinkles simply are not allowed. But those wrinkles should be a badge of honor. Look how long it took us to earn every one of them. Every wrinkle signifies added wisdom. In this youth-oriented culture, trying to compete is difficult.

Many female Hollywood stars find work very hard to come by after 40. With the aging of America, perhaps things will change—but I don't expect much when I see men in their 50s and 60s dating women in their 30s and 40s. The need to stay young and look young has been forced on us. The emphasis on youth and beauty makes life especially hard for a woman who does not understand she is much more than just a pretty face. She must see she has a mind and a soul. It is the nurturing of the soul that will do more to keep her beautiful throughout her life than any $100 miracle cream or cosmetic makeover.

You can easily cover your entire body with boots, pants, turtleneck sweaters, scarves, long sleeves, and gloves. But it is your face and eyes that shine out from your camouflaged body. Your face reflects how you feel and it's your face that tells your story. Is it reasonable to be concerned with the appearance of your face? Is it wrong or egotistical for you to want to put your best face forward? Absolutely not! Bright eyes and a cheerful, joyful, attractive face are what God desires for you. People of joy are mentioned 50 times in the Bible. A stunning face filled with gratitude and joy is a beautiful sight to behold!

There are circumstances in life completely out of our control: recessions, interest rates, corporate downsizing, our height, our eye and skin colors. But there is a long list of conditions and attitudes that *do* fall under our control. These are our education, finances, food and drink choices, our weight and career choices, our personal success with relationships, our daily decisions, and definitely our grooming, style, body care, and image.

I will never forget a girl in my high school so many years ago. She was similar to me in height, six feet, and model thin. She had not been blessed with a bone structure that would classify her as beautiful or even pretty. However, by choice, attractive she truly was. She stood out in any crowd as being one of the most beautifully groomed. What she lacked in physical beauty, she made up for in intelligence, composure, and her ability to pay close attention to detail.

It was a daily pleasure to see her perfectly groomed and coordinated head to toe. She stood tall and walked with dignity, confidence, and grace. I heard years later she married a successful company president who sought a beautifully groomed, magnificent woman. What she lacked in physical beauty, she made up for in every other way. Any woman can be stunningly attractive because beauty is more than bone structure, tight skin, and thin thighs. It does take time, thought, and care, but aren't you worth it? Of course you are.

My school classmate walked and talked beautifully, dressed and groomed herself beautifully, and developed a reputation as a beautiful woman inside and out. God has, in his love for you, anointed you as perfect in his eyes. Honor him, not only with the beauty of your soul, but also with your mind and body.

A heart at peace gives life to the body,
but envy rots the bones.
—PROVERBS 14:30 NIV

Eighty Years of Inspiration

A few years ago I ended up in the hospital for eight days. The hospital has a chaplain and numerous volunteers who would drop by to visit. One day a delightful man with a physique to rival Mister America's came to visit me. He stood straight as a board with no shoulder droop or belly pooch. He was also tanned with silver hair and was dressed with style. As we began to chat, he told me his daily exercise routine. I was impressed and asked him about his occupation, assuming he was 50-something. He said he had been retired for years—as he was 80 years old! My mouth dropped open in shock, and I'm sure this happened to him on a daily basis. He was the best-looking advertisement for exercise, having a positive attitude, and their effect on anti-aging I had ever seen; he was a hydrated, oxygenated, exercising anti-aging machine. He traveled from room to room, spreading God's love and encouragement to all who needed comforting. I do not remember his name, but I will never forget him. His mind, body, and soul were in harmony with one another and the world.

According to the *Consumers Report Magazine* in September 2010 Americans are now spending over 30 billion dollars on dietary supplements. In addition they spend 4.7 billion on multi-vitamins with no proof they improve a persons health. Add tothis the comsumption of over 16 thousand tons of aspirin and over 15 billion tranquilizers, amphetamines and barbiturates,and at last count over 68% of U.S. population take something in hopes they will feel better, live longer lives, or stave off aging. Many people are looking for a youth pill or lotion, and unscrupulous companies pop up each year more than happy to oblige. A pushy marketing company can make millions of dollars before the FDA moves in. Just how many new diets and diet pills have been introduced in the past twenty-five years? There are no magic pills yet, and there are no magic creams that will stop the aging process. However, the aging process *can* be slowed with some mental, physical, and spiritual lifestyle changes.

People with few financial limitations are spending upwards of $1,200 a year on anti-aging prescription programs, injections, and/or hormone therapy. Spend all you want, but I still have never seen a 70-year-old with the body or face of a 30-year-old. Can you totally stop the aging process? Yes—die in your sleep tonight. But there are things you can do to *slow* aging. You may initially think my ideas unconventional, but they have worked for me and my family.

The *most* successful anti-aging program is one that begins early in life. Those who take advantage of it are the women you meet who look like their grown child's older sibling. Women who took the road less traveled; those who made a total commitment to nurture their personal as well as their spiritual lives; women who found a loving God ever present through the tears of sadness and joy.

Most people I have interviewed want more: more beauty, more money, more of everything. The list is endless when it comes to wanting more. Incredibly, I find they haven't yet made the most of what they already have. In his Word, God tells us he has given us all we need, yet we want more. Concentrate on doing your best with what you have been given.

Eighty-three percent of people base their first impression of a person on sight, 11 percent on hearing, 3.5 percent on smell, 1.5 percent on touch. Even more significant is the fact that those decisions are generally made in the first 30 seconds. Of the 83 percent who judge by sight, 55 percent are primarily influenced by body language, says Lynda Goldman, author of "How to Make a Million-Dollar First Impression." God gave us our five senses not only for our enjoyment but to also help us make discerning decisions.

The Gift of Health

Beauty comes from a deep spring that floods the body with spiritual hope, faith, and love. Nothing is more beautiful than the face of a woman who knows how to love and who feels love all around her. Love—true, unconditional love—results in happiness, and there is little that surpasses the beauty of a happy face.

Making your health and body among your top priorities
is one of the most giving and loving gifts you can give
your spouse, yourself, and your children.

An acquaintance, now in her early 60s, is a full-time caregiver to her husband of the same age who can do nothing for himself. He suffered a debilitating stroke. This man abused his health with an overabundance of unhealthy living during their entire married life. Who is paying the price for his actions? His wife. His selfish attitude has hurt the people he was supposed to have loved and cared for. Be wise, show character, and take care of yourself. Character is your ability to carry out a resolution long after the mood in which it was made has passed. Your character is your dominant quality.

If you sincerely want to succeed in slowing down the aging process, you must have character. You must have the character to stick to a diet and/or limit your calories, stick to an exercise program, and eliminate unhealthy habits. Develop the character to make positive decisions for your life.

Your character will greatly influence the lines you will carry on your face. Your character is the sum total of *all* your habits. If you make it a habit to put on sunscreen and wear sunglasses every time you are in the sun; if you make it a habit to be positive rather than negative, to develop faith rather than live in fear, and to love rather than hate; and if you make it a habit to say "No, thank you" to dessert and white bread, then you will reap the benefits. If you make sure your skin is free of all traces of makeup before bed and you daily use a moisturizer, you are developing great habits that will be rewarding in the long term. Keep in mind there are no instant habits. Repetition is the mother of all sound habits, skills, and character.

With faith, character, and wholesome habits over your lifetime, you can win the aging game. This minute you have the opportunity to make a decision to determine your personal success and future in the area of anti-aging. The younger you are, the more likely you will be to break all the rules for anti-aging success; so listen up and muster a little character and form habits that will do wonders for your face and health throughout your life.

In time, your character will establish your reputation, and your reputation will determine the respect you receive (or the lack thereof).

Time-Tested Beauty

For attractive lips, speak words of kindness.

For lovely eyes, seek out the good in people.

For a slim figure, share your food with the hungry.

For beautiful hair, let a child run his fingers through it once a day.

For poise, walk with the knowledge you'll never walk alone.

The tender, loving care of human beings will never become obsolete.

People, even more than things, need to be restored, renewed,
    revived, reclaimed, and redeemed and redeemed and
    redeemed.

Never throw out anybody.

And remember, if you ever need a helping hand, you'll find one at
    the end of your arm.

As you grow older, you will discover you have two hands: one for
    helping yourself, the other for helping others.

Your "good old days" are still ahead of you—may you have many.

—AUDREY HEPBURN

Charm is deceptive, and beauty is fleeting;
but a woman who fears the LORD is to be praised.
—PROVERBS 31:30 NIV

Part Two

IT ALL BEGINS WITH A STRONG FOUNDATION

Stone One:
How Strong
Is Your Foundation?

One of the most important aspects of an age-defying life is a foundation that will withstand life's pressure, a foundation so strong that, no matter what happens in your life, good or bad, that foundation will not crack. Would you go to the top of the Sears Tower or the Empire State Building if you knew they were not bolted down to a strong foundation? Shortly before Marilyn Monroe's death she stated she knew she had a great superstructure but no foundation. Often people go through life never considering the foundation of their own life. I attribute a great deal of my personal anti-aging success to my beliefs in establishing that foundation. The stones in your foundation must be made of granite.

The first stone is knowing clearly your purpose and your principles. You were put on Earth not by accident but by design. Read, study, and grow. It is a proven fact that people with faith and purpose are healthier, happier, and live longer, perhaps because they know their mission on Earth is to serve. Be precise on the principles and ethics that will define all your decisions. This first stone must be cast in bedrock. Once you know unequivocally what principles you stand for and your purpose for being here on Earth, stand firm. It makes decision making so much easier. Years ago a man walked into my office and offered me twice what I had paid for it. He threw down a paper bag containing many thousands of dollars from a slush fund he was hiding from the IRS. He wanted an under-the-table deal. After accepting the cash initially, I was so guilt-ridden I returned every cent. This offer was most tempting but caused many sleepless nights. I wonder how many guilt lines I would have had over the fear the IRS would one night drag me out of my bed and into jail had I decided to take the offer. I stood strong on my foundation and principles and said no. Life is the sum of all your experiences, thoughts, and personal growth—grow a little each day by doing the right thing.

One of the most popular books published in the past decade, *The Purpose Driven Life* by Rick Warren, has been purchased by millions. Does this indicate most people are unsure as to what life's true purpose is? Why are we here? If you have not read Rick Warren's book I suggest you do. Perhaps it will help you define your purpose.

The first two elements to be defined as parts of a strong anti-aging foundation are your purpose and the set of principles that will drive your life forward. They are the first two pieces of life's puzzle. Life often feels like a giant jigsaw puzzle—confusing and fragmented, but with time and patience, the pieces fit together creating a beautiful existence.

God put us on this earth to serve out his purpose for our lives. Challenges are his way of showing us that purpose. Trust that God indeed has a plan and purpose for your life. He will most likely present his plan to you by challenging you. Think about Moses, David, or Job. This I will promise you: submitting to God's plan and purpose will put a spring in your step and a smile on your face, and you will have more fun than you can imagine.

Stone Two:
Rock-Solid Standards

The next stone represents your personal standards. What are your standards? Have you clearly defined them in your mind? If so, have you taken a piece of paper and written them down? Writing helps to make standards real and clear in your mind's eye and easier to achieve.

Personally, I will not, if it can be avoided, ride around in a dirty automobile. It may seem silly, but my standards are my own, as your standards are of your choosing.

I will not go to bed with makeup on my face, even if it's 3 a.m. and I am exhausted from travel.

I will wear leather shoes, eat meat, and wear fur if I want to. Things will never be more important than people. I will dress with elegance and dignity at all times.

My home will be a smoke-free zone.

I consider myself intelligent enough to never use foul language. The dictionary is full of words that can take the place of bad language.

My living standards will reflect my personal standards—clean, neat, uncluttered, and well-kept.

My home will be open to all people: saints and sinners, and people from all nations, cultures, and backgrounds.

Every day I will express words of praise to better someone's life.

Shakespeare wrote, in *Hamlet*, "Unto thine own self be true." Good advice!

Each day try to give someone a compliment that requires a "thank you" response. Every time you reach out to make another person feel good, her body reacts, and responds to the positive stimulus. Start with your husband, child, friend, or a stranger. For the next two-week period, criticize no one. Do not make one personal negative comment to or about anyone. These two simple acts will be like a TNT anti-aging explosion for your body and your face.

Stone Three: Future Fundamentals

The next stone for your life's anti-aging foundation is to write your goal list, everything you desire to achieve through your own efforts. Little is as uplifting to your self-esteem as accomplishing the goals you have set for yourself. Jesus said he came to give us life—an abundant life—so take him up on his offer.

There are different reasons people strive to accomplish their goals. For some it's power, for others it's the feeling of accomplishment or achievement, and for others it's the satisfaction they get through love and relationships. In order to make good on your list of goals, you must have someone you want to do it for.

> *The greatest moments in life are not concerned with selfish*
> *achievements but rather with the things we do for the people*
> *we love and esteem and those whose respect we need.*
> —Walter Elias Disney

Whatever success I have had or will have in the future, the person I wish to please is my heavenly Father, as nothing else truly matters. Many years ago I sat down and wrote my lifetime goal list. I had twenty-five items on my list. With God as my business partner, I have only one yet to fulfill.

If Helen Keller, who was blind and deaf, traveled the country giving speeches, I have to believe God can help you with your dreams and goals. Irving Berlin had only two years of formal schooling, never took a music lesson, never learned to read music, and yet he had a goal to give the world some of its most beautiful music. No matter your age, if you are alive, that is reason enough to set a new goal. Having something to strive toward keeps us young. I believe in re-inventing myself on a regular basis. I take walks and have talks with God and ask him, "Okay, what's next?" The result of one of those walks and talks is *Anti-Aging God's Way.*

Your goals and/or success may have little to do with money. It was not money that made Mother Teresa famous. It was the riches of serving God and mankind that brought her happiness and wealth of the heart. Happiness is the best goal one can achieve. When it comes to anti-aging, you are always in a position to set a goal. You can decide to do something, or you can decide to do nothing. It's not your will power that will bring you success—it's your "want" power.

The greatest gift God ever gave you was the gift of free choice. The first principle of goal success is desire. After all is said and done, each of us is the architect of her own life. Through the words in this book, I am here as a coach to help encourage you to be more fabulous than you already may be. Defining new goals at every age and stage of your life is exciting and rewarding, and keeps you young. Remember—anti-aging is as much attitude as expensive cosmetics or treatments. To truly succeed, seek God's will for your life.

Success has an effect on your aging agenda. Just as you must have all the ingredients in the exact proportions to create the perfect pastry, you must also combine all the components in the proper amounts to create a life of fulfillment, happiness, satisfaction, and joy. My goal is for you to see and contemplate the common thread that weaves itself throughout the lives of people who have mastered the techniques that result in a lifetime of success and youthfulness.

You can have success in your efforts to slow the aging process, success at work, success in marriage, success with relationships. Visit your local Barnes and Noble bookstore and you will find an entire section dedicated to success—from sex to selling, from relationships to real estate. Most often, however, the word *success* is used as an indication of one's bank balance.

I was standing on a large stage just behind the curtain, listening to a motivational speaker as I waited for my turn at the podium. I listened intently as he listed ten items that indicated one's personal success. I began to realize his criteria for success showed that only money mattered—without it you had completely failed.

As I continued to listen, I became so upset it affected the quality of my own presentation. What I desperately wanted to do was run on stage and scream, "He is so wrong!" By his criteria my own husband—one of the sweetest, most loving husbands a woman could ever hope for—would be defined as a failure. Like many loving, serving, giving people on this earth, the accumulation of money has never been the primary focus of my husband's life. His true spiritual gift is service. I decided at that moment I would set out to determine the true and complete definition of the word *success*.

I learned that success is the realization of a worthy goal. Any goal you set and accomplish qualifies you as a successful person. Most of the people I have met throughout my journey in life are far more successful than they realize, once money is no longer considered the only measure of success.

When I met Dean, he was contemplating suicide. He had grown up in a very verbally abusive home in the South. Now an adult and unable to read or write, he was ready to give up on life, believing all the negative statements spoken to him as a child. As we talked, I discovered he had a talent for taking beautiful pictures. I redirected his thinking away from what he could not do to what he *could* do. Has he become successful? He has raised three beautiful children, has a loving wife, and lives comfortably. Is he rich in wealth? No. Is he rich in life? Yes.

Some of you have dealt with the painful loss of a child or spouse or have been faced with personal illness or addiction, but you have made it. In my eyes, you have success written all over your face.

According to motivational speaker Zig Ziglar (my speaking partner on the Masters of Success Rallies), a survey of college graduates indicated that only 10 percent of college students clearly define their lifetime goals. Of that 10 percent, only half write them down on paper and review them regularly. *Of the 5 percent of people who make and write down their goal list, all 5 percent succeed!*

Right down your goal list. Not having a goal is *not* acceptable. Whether large or small, a goal moves us forward. Write your long-term and short-term goals, and check on your progress regularly.

Success God's Way

Success is to *surmount*.
Success is to *triumph*.
Success is to *overcome*.
Success is to *conquer*.
Success is to *master*.
Success is to *defeat*.
Success is to *win*.
Success is to *flourish*.
Success is to *thrive*.
Success is to *bloom*.
Success is to *prosper*.
Success is to *advance*.
Success is to *progress*.
Success is to *accomplish*.
Success is to *reap*.
Success is to *complete*.

*I have fought a good fight, I have finished the race,
and I have remained faithful. And now the prize awaits me.*
—2 TIMOTHY 4:7–8 NLT

Go back over your list, and check off the many accomplishments you have achieved in your life. Then, and only then, will you realize just how successful you have been. I tell you these things because that wonderful feeling of accomplishment shines in your eyes and shows on your face. *It is one of the connecting knots in the thread of life that slows aging.* It will show in the way you carry yourself, the way you walk, and the way you hold your head. Body language speaks volumes. My father's goal at 94 was to live to be one hundred. That is why you saw him at the gym three days a week.

To remain young in heart, mind, and soul, you must know your goal. Wake up every day with optimism and positive expectancy, nurture your relationship with God, and have faith that he did not make a mistake when you were born. Put it all together and you will exude youth and happiness. God has given you the ability to make a living and a life. What you choose to do with both is your decision. However, if you have chosen fear over faith, there is not much God can do to help you accomplish your heart's desire.

The Ultimate Goal List

1. Contentment
2. Peace of mind
3. Freedom from guilt
4. No fear of the future
5. Someone to love

There you have a great recipe for eliminating worry lines on your face and stress from your heart. If you love and have been loved, my precious one, you are very successful. I challenge you, no matter your present age—do something. Do something with your talent, do something with your knowledge and experience, do something with that idea you have had for 30 years. Get out of that Lazy Boy and go for it! A spring of youth will flow through those veins. Develop an intense desire to accomplish a new goal. Goals are what keep us going. Goals challenge us. *Goals are anti-aging.* When you succeed at one goal, set a new one, and you will always have something exciting to look forward to. If you set a goal and it does not come to fruition, oh, well, who cares? Set a new goal and try again.

Jonas Salk came up with 200 serums before he found one that prevented polio. Macy failed seven times before he put together a store that succeeded. Babe Ruth, known for hitting home runs, struck out 1,330 times. Did these men quit or feel like failures? No, they simply acknowledged they had made a mistake, or messed up, or had a false start, or a glitch or an error, but they never saw themselves as failures. They, as do we all, learned twice as much from their mistakes as they did from success.

If you live with passion, you will always project youth. Find something you feel passionate about. Then develop a plan and persist. Colonel Sanders enjoyed cooking chicken and at the age of 65, he developed a new process and started his now-famous chain of restaurants. And the Colonel indeed died a young man at an old age.

For Excitement—
Take Risks

As my boss carefully explained, I had reached the glass ceiling. I had maxed out the income level for my position at Disneyland at the age of 42. That's an age when far too many people do not embrace risk as an option for their lives and opt for what is comfortable, familiar, and secure. If I had been single, I must assume and hope I would have decided to take the same chance and risk starting my company and following my dream. My husband made it clear he could not finance my little venture so I would have to go it alone.

As I write this page, I am sitting in the Auckland, New Zealand, airport, having just arrived from Los Angeles. In a few short hours I will arrive in Queenstown, New Zealand, my destination for this week. Last week I was in Vancouver, Canada, and a few weeks ago in Singapore, Hong Kong, Bali, and Australia. I am not telling you this to impress you or depress you or fill up my own ego. I am giving you this information to let you know that taking that risk of leaving a secure job with all its benefits has led me on an adventure far greater than I could ever have imagined, *and* I accomplished one of my early goals.

I am not one of the wealthiest women in America or the most famous, but I'm convinced I am one of the happiest and most personally fulfilled women in my area. Risking what is comfortable, financially secure, and permanent can be scary at times, and exhausting at other times. It can also be the ultimate challenge of our self-confidence. It can build or at times bruise our self-esteem, depending on the win-or-lose factor. However, the one thing risking will never be is dull. Risking is adventure; it is exciting, and it will challenge you far beyond your present comprehension of yourself. The ability to risk what you have in exchange for what you want is an attitude, an attribute, not all people possess.

The two women who published my first book combined two small publishing houses to form what they hoped would be a major player in the field of publishing. Were they scared? Yes. They, too, questioned if giving up their successful law careers was the right move. But putting all that aside, the adventure was worth it—it was fun for them. And they accomplished their goal.

What does it take to risk? *Faith in God and belief in yourself.* Those two things are more important than your education, your financial situation, your background, or your appearance. I recall the day I felt I was earning enough money to warrant a financial counselor. I contacted my husband's friend, a president of a savings and loan institution. My question was, "What should I do with my money?" After discussing my situation with him, I determined to continue to develop courage to risk and enjoy the thrill—the thrill of risking it all for adventure. I advise you to do the same, if adventure is what you want.

The Final Stone: Your Personal Philosophy

The final stone in your foundation is your personal philosophy. My philosophy is *to live a guilt-free life.* When I was part of the Disney Company, I became aware of the power of a philosophy. Disney's philosophy was "We create happiness." You could change that to "I create happiness." That would make a wonderful philosophy for anyone. How about "I will trust God in all things"? Others could be "I will live with passion and purpose" or "I will live my life with a sense of joy through God's example of unconditional love." I also like, "The only reason to have children is to enjoy them." (That one is for you stressed-out moms.)

Develop a philosophy that will bless you and those around you with happiness and joy. Courage to live life to the fullest comes from faith. Faith is the opposite of fear, and the Bible tells us 366 times to not be afraid. Develop a philosophy that gives you the courage to endure all that life throws at you.

I was driving with my older daughter on our way to lunch when I told her how wonderful it was to be at an age and place in my life where I felt I had nothing to prove. My daughter said she could hardly wait to get to that point in her life. We all have dreams and, like you, I wanted very badly to see my dream list become reality. It was not that I had a need to prove anything to anyone. I just wanted to prove to myself I could achieve what I set out to accomplish. As I look back and review my life, God's fingerprints are all over it. He opened the doors, and I chose to enter, swallowing my fear and trepidation. Every time I did, he presented me with another door more thrilling than the last. What is the reasoning behind developing an unyielding life foundation? Clarity, strength, steadfastness, and faithfulness to the clear vision of who you are eliminates hours of stress and confusion. As an example, you may own your dream car; however, if the tires are flat, the car is not functional. All areas of your foundation must be fully functioning, clear, and solid as a rock for you to age gracefully, elegantly, and slowly.

A methodical, well-thought-out life foundation, along with balance, will eliminate body stress and increase soul contentment. Life functions to its fullest when all systems are working in support of one another. Until you can easily explain your purpose for being here on Earth, the principles that back up your every decision, the daily standards by which you will live your life, and your lifetime philosophy, goals, desires, and dreams, you are like a ship without a rudder, just drifting through life. Don't just let life happen—*make* it happen! Constantly open yourself up to the adventures of life.

My Personal List

Purpose: To serve the Lord.

Principles: To live by the Golden Rule.

Standards: To respect myself by always doing my personal best in all things.

Philosophy: To lead a guilt-free life.

Goal: To never allow fear to keep me from accomplishing my dreams.

Every Day . . .

1. Accomplish something.
2. Exercise at least 30 minutes.
3. Be thankful for what you have accomplished.
4. Brighten the life of another person.
5. Do some mental exercise.
6. Be kind to yourself.
7. Set something aside for the future.
8. Drink sixty to eighty ounces of water.
9. Become more proficient at living.
10. Present yourself professionally.

Part Three

THE FIRST STEPS TO ANTI-AGING SUCCESS

The Fruits of a Positive Attitude

The first negative signs of aging are due to our failing muscular system. Gravity is pulling those muscles down 24/7, and gravity wins the tug-o-war every time. One great advantage of being six feet tall is that my breasts have a long way to go to reach my waist. Our body has muscles, our face has muscles—why is it that our face can show emotion, but our knees cannot? The muscles in our body are attached to our bones, but the muscles of our face are attached to our skin, and that is the reason our face shows every emotion we feel. With the emotional makeup of a female, our facial muscles get a daily workout. Happiness or sadness, conflicts or resolutions, bitterness or forgiveness, minute by minute, day by day, our attitude and thoughts are affecting how we will look twenty-five years from now. This is surprising—but true.

A new acquaintance from my church told me she had been attending divorce recovery classes and shared with me how shocked she was by the amount of bitterness in the women. She said, "I have every right to be bitter with what happened to me, but I refuse to allow it to destroy me. I will move forward as best I can." Her positive attitude is reflected in her lovely unlined face.

At 17 and fresh out of high school, I was hired to teach personal improvement and modeling at the largest John Robert Powers Studio in America. As I look back on my life, it seems surreal to me. I see now that God definitely had a plan for my life. My students ranged from young teenagers to women in their 70s. I taught poise, modeling, skin care, and makeup classes in Pasadena, California, and then in San Francisco. Some women came just for fun, but many came due to disappointments in life.

I learned what emotional pain and stress can do to a once-beautiful woman. I studied the faces of women in pain and those filled with the joy that comes from the knowledge of a loving God. The faces of women who lived their lives with no hope had wrinkles—as did the women who had lived lives of faith and a commitment to God. But the first group's wrinkles carried hard edges while the second group's faces, even though wrinkled, looked soft and pretty. Successful aging and depth of beauty is indeed an inside-out proposition. This is a simple yet true fact.

Nutritionists say, "We are what we eat," but I say we are what we believe and what we believe in and what we will or will not stand for in our lives. We all have desires, and besides looking beautiful at age 65, we have a desire for good health. We desire honest, peaceful, loving relationships. We desire praise and appreciation, personal and business success. We desire time for rest and relaxation, and all of us on this earth desire peace, peace of mind, and freedom from frustration, anxiety, fear, and worry. To worry is human nature, but worry is also a waste of time because 95 percent of what we worry about never happens. Twelve times the Bible cautions us not to worry.

During the Sermon on the Mount, Jesus commanded us to trust him completely for all our needs (Matthew 6:25–33). That means stop worrying, start praying, and trust that God will show you his compassion.

A woman who desires lasting beauty inside and outside must take a trip into her feelings and the emotional baggage she is carrying around year in and year out. One of the reasons to embrace God's teachings is the knowledge that people who have wronged you will one day stand before the Lord. No one gets away without that last judgment. That has been comforting to me throughout my life. I have learned to let God deal in his way with an offender. Use that confirmation to save your face from lines of resentment, bitterness, and anger. Every face is a masterpiece, and God is the Artist.

We have all heard, "Attitude is everything." I am a firm believer in this philosophy. Attitude is an often-overlooked quality that has a powerful influence on aging. One of the most important principles to develop in your life is the need for a positive attitude. Personally, I find it very unpleasant to be around negative people. They tire me out and drag me down. I do my best to avoid their negativism.

How you will age depends to a great extent on your attitude, and how you view life in general. I personally choose not to live in negative reality. I choose to focus on the wonder, beauty, and happiness of life. I have been told I do not live in reality because I pick positive over negative every time I have a choice. The only thing you accomplish with a negative attitude is failure. Positive attitudes bring positive results, whether it is your work, your family, your health, or the condition of your face.

Some people heal at a rate I can only explain in two ways; (1) a miracle due to prayer, or (2) an extremely positive attitude. The brain is in control. Our brain sets into motion hundreds of thousands of chemical combinations per second related to our emotions, thoughts, or attitude at that second. New studies have come to light showing that the body we imagine may be the body we will have. Research is looking into the mind's ability to change body shape.

I recall a story concerning a man with multiple personality disorder. One of his personalities was that of a ladies' man. Another was a serious, self-conscious, unattractive man. For me, one of the most shocking side effects of this disorder was that his studious personality needed glasses, but his outgoing, womanizing side could see fine without glasses.

My friend U.S. Navy Captain (Retired) Gerald Coffee told me an amazing story of attitude and faith. Held for seven years in the Hanoi Hilton prisoner-of-war camp during the Vietnam War, he said, "A positive attitude saved my life. The prisoners who lost faith in themselves, faith in their country, and faith in God, all died. But those who kept their faith in their country, themselves, and God survived." Never forget you hold within you an inexhaustible reservoir of possibilities and abilities only partially touched.

Is there more to staying and looking young than attitude, emotional health, stress reduction, and casting your cares toward Heaven? That calls for a great big *yes*. Without proper physical exercise, healthy nutrition, and a total commitment to skin care you will not be completely successful. Remember—*Anti-Aging God's Way* is three-dimensional (body, mind, and soul), so we must address the reality of and the responsibility we have to our body. But never forget that attitude comes before achievement.

According to Hall of Fame basketball coach John Wooden, "Things turn out best for the people who make the best of the way things turn out." When it comes to accepting life as it is, few people beat my friend W. Mitchell. He found himself in a fire ten feet high and four feet wide after being struck on his motorcycle by a truck. He survived, but his hands and face were so badly burned and disfigured that children feared him.

He moved to a small town in Colorado. He explained to everyone what happened and eventually became a very successful businessman, so successful he purchased his own plane. One day, while taking clients to see property, his plane reached only one hundred feet, then crashed. Fearing fire, he yelled for everyone to exit the plane and run. It was then he realized he could not move. His back was broken.

First he was burned, and then he lost his ability to walk! But Mitchell decided to take the high road, and for years has motivated people to understand that it is not what happens in life, but how you respond to what happens, that counts.

Keeping the Faith

Ann lost her beautiful home, her car, and most of the amenities money can buy. What she never lost, however, was her acceptance of her situation, her upbeat attitude, her faith in God, and the decision to think positively. That attitude has had an amazing effect on her friends. People are now asking her the question: From where does this attitude come? For Ann and many others, happiness is the result of joy, and joy is what you get when you know beyond a shadow of a doubt that you are one of God's children. He has your best interest at heart. God knows what you are facing. God knows all your needs, problems, and fears. All the muscles in your face can relax when you know the Master of Heaven and Earth is on your side. Ann has suffered much the past five years, but, like Job in the Bible, her faith in a loving God allows her to remain beautiful inside and out.

The Essence of Beauty Is Happiness

Live in a state of perpetual happiness as much as is reasonable. I am not talking about a state of ignorance, denial, or pretend, but if you have a choice, choose happy. What is truly more beautiful than happiness? People who do not smile disturb me greatly. In one of my Bible study small groups, there is a woman who never smiles. Her mouth turns down, and she looks years older than her actual age. Due to her negativity, I find I tend to avoid her. Abraham Lincoln said, "We will be as happy as we choose to be." Happy, positive people have different immune responses to viruses, too, and therefore remain healthier.

Case in point: Funny man Art Buchwald lived years beyond his medically predicted life span, full of humor up to the day he died. Laughing and humor are affirmations of man's superiority over all other living creatures. God gave his children the gift of laughter, and with laughter, comes happiness. Happy people have healthier levels of key body chemicals in their daily lives than people who are not happy. Happy people have been found to have lower levels of cortisol, a stress hormone linked to hypertension.

Happiness: delight, gladness, good spirits, playfulness, rejoicing, exhilaration, gratification, hopefulness, and peace. These are only nine words out of the more than one hundred I found to define *happiness*.

Your personal happiness may be hard to define, but you know it when it's there. Many people worldwide come to the United States in the pursuit of happiness, yet millions of U.S.-born citizens have never achieved a feeling of complete happiness. If you desire the beauty of a happy face, never forget that happiness is a choice. With every situation you face every day of your life, *you* choose your emotional response.

A Person Is Happier When She:

1. takes full responsibility for herself.
2. seeks wisdom, and acts in that wisdom.
3. takes responsibility for her health—exercising and eating properly.
4. has given herself permission to like and accept herself just as she is.
5. takes responsibility for her future.
6. sets and achieves goals.
7. has a positive self-image.
8. accepts challenges.
9. lives full of self-assurance and confidence.
10. has strong, loving relationships.
11. has an active social life.
12. is part of God's family.
13. trusts God completely.
14. has self-respect.
15. is surrounded by positive people.
16. doesn't compare herself with others.
17. is comfortable with her appearance and weight.
18. accepts her imperfections.
19. gives of herself.
20. chooses love.
21. overflows with gratitude.
22. is using her full potential.
23. knows her purpose for being on Earth.

24. is overcoming life's difficulties.
25. is working toward a worthy goal.

Put a check by each statement you feel represents you at the beginning of your journey in *Anti-Aging God's Way*. When you finish reading the book, return to see if you have changed your thinking.

Living in Abundance

> *Jesus said, "I am come that they*
> *might have life, and that they might*
> *have it more abundantly."*
> —JOHN 10:10 KJV

To have an abundant, free, happy life you must first feel deserving of such a life. Beauty and youth come from a deep spring that floods the body with spiritual hope, faith, and love. Contentment is on the face of a woman who knows how to love and who feels love all around her. Love—true, unconditional love—results in happiness, and there is little that surpasses what happiness can do for one's health.

The word *happiness* comes from the Greek word *hap*, as in *happenstance*. For some, happiness levels increase or decrease depending on circumstances. Others have made a decision to be happy no matter what the circumstances. Try to find the positive in the negative, to concentrate on the good in people, including yourself. Women who develop an optimistic view of their lives always age at a slower pace. When we are happy, we think better, feel better, perform better, and sleep better. Our physical organs work better. When we are happy, our five senses are intensified and our memory is improved. Happy people are not mean, ugly, or evil. Women who look for the bright side in all situations have a light that continually shines through their eyes.

At age 42, I began a new phase of my life. I am far from being wealthy, but by focusing my attention on God, my goals, and happiness, I began a new adventure. I could have stayed in my secure position as Disneyland's Image Coordinator and retired with a nice pension. I traded the security of a pension for the dream of adventure. My wonderful husband advised me to follow my dreams. Together we reap the rewards, and as a result, we share many happy memories of our worldwide travels. When the time is right, follow your dream.

Happiness means "a condition of supreme well-being and good spirits." The end result, a happy woman, is always a beautiful woman.

Many people are on a quest for happiness. They explore diverse avenues but untold numbers agree finding God and the security of Heaven has brought them the most profound, incredible, commanding peace of body, mind, and soul they have ever known.

Happiness is a *powerful concentration of anti-aging antibiotics*.
Happiness is a *muscle relaxer*.
Happiness is an *antidepressant*.
Happiness *segregates you from many illnesses*.

A recent documentary that focused on aging and longevity featured two groups of centenarians. One group of one-hundred-year-olds had lived a life of reckless abandon, paying little attention to healthy living. The second group had lived a more conservative life, giving thought to lifestyle and health issues. The two groups shared two common threads: good genes and happiness. Both groups acknowledged having been very happy throughout their hundred years.

My own husband eats more foods containing high volumes of sugar than any person I know. Yet he has never been sick, and he is not overweight. He is physically active, has a deep calmness in his soul, and is a *happy person*. Why is he so healthy? Perhaps it is his great character, peace of mind, and overall emotional health. Certainly, it is not his diet.

In November of 2006, Reuters published the results of a study on happiness and health, conducted by Dr. Sheldon Cohen of Carnegie Mellon University. The report stated that staying positive could be your best defense against getting sick. In an experiment that exposed healthy volunteers to cold or flu viruses, researchers found that people with generally sunny, happy dispositions were less likely to become ill. They concluded positive emotions can help ward off not only the common cold but other illnesses as well. People with a positive emotional outlook may have different immune responses to cold and flu viruses.

Negative feelings such as anger and anxiety cause a chain reaction in the body. The brain produces more stress hormones, blood pressure rises, and blood vessels constrict. The heart beats erratically or skips a beat intermittently. The emotional centers of the brain receive these erratic patterns and analyze them as stressful and negative.

"Love and positive emotions create a different cycle. Heart rhythms synch in harmony, and an efficient cardio-vascular system prompts the brain to send out signals of pleasure, well-being and reward." (Body World)

The Seven Wonders of the World

This fabulous story was sent to me from Maria Ying Matthews, who lives in China.

A group of students were asked what would make their list of the Seven Wonders of the World. The following received the most votes:

1. Egypt's Great Pyramids
2. Taj Mahal
3. Grand Canyon
4. Panama Canal
5. Empire State Building
6. St.Peter's Basilica
7. Great Wall of China

While gathering the questionnaires, the teacher noted that one student had not yet finished. So she asked the girl if she was having trouble with her list. The girl replied, "Yes, a little. I couldn't make up my mind because there are so many." The teacher said "Well, tell us what you have and maybe we can help."

The girl hesitated, and then read, "I think the Seven Wonders of the World are:

1. To see
2. To hear
3. To touch
4. To taste
5. To feel
6. To laugh
7. And to love."

The room was so quiet you could hear a pin drop. The things we overlook as simple or ordinary, and that we often take for granted, are truly wondrous. It was a gentle reminder the most precious and important gifts in life are already ours, and that these gifts were given to us by our Maker.

Despite your feelings toward yourself, you are a masterful piece of art with a heart. Each day, be grateful for the wondrous gifts you have been given. Untie the ribbon, and enjoy the gifts with a thankful heart. Although we desire to confront the world with an attractive appearance, life is so much more than an unlined face.

In the story of the Seven Wonders of the World, the girl who read her list will most likely always recognize happiness. She is grateful for the things most people take for granted, and at the age of 60, she will probably look 45. This young child already understands the principles of happiness and gratitude. Happy people live rich, full lives. Happy people are more relaxed.

Impatient people are critical of themselves and others. Impatient people honk, yell, drum their fingers, tap their toes, lose their temper, and use up energy stupidly. Impatient people are prone to ill health, high blood pressure, heart attacks, and rapid aging.

The Two Most Powerful Forces on Earth: the Human Brain and the Human Heart

Our success will be driven by our deepest desire, as desire is the key to success. It is desire that creates its own motivation. Our bodies respond to our brain, so start talking to yourself. Tell yourself how beautiful, thin, healthy, and fabulous you are. In this day and age of cell phones and other electronic headgear, you can talk out loud to yourself without even a glance from others wondering if you're on the edge of insanity.

After I finished a presentation in the state of Washington, a man named Michael approached me and said he would like to share his story on the power of visual imaging, brain control, and the effect of attitude on the human body. He said as a boy he witnessed his father's death. A few years later, he witnessed President John F. Kennedy's assassination, and shortly thereafter, saw seven of his fellow recruits die while preparing to leave for Vietnam.

Michael told me his brain short-circuited and just shut down. Michael lost complete control of all his bodily functions. He could no longer walk, hear, or see, as his eyes had moved too far to the right. He became a human vegetable. He said, "One day I realized I could still think, and that the one thing I could do was try to control my brain." Michael began to visualize his former self and demanded his brain respond to those images. It took a number of years and then Michael said, "Here I am." Due to atrophy in his leg muscles, Michael used crutches, but he could see, hear, walk, and talk with only slight difficulty. He said, "I pictured, I dreamed, and I talked to my brain. I knew my brain had the power to give me a renewed body."

Michael proved to me the power the brain has over our bodies. Our brain is "master control," so I developed an anti-aging routine based on that knowledge. When driving, I talk to my brain. If this sounds weird to you, it is no different than programming your home computer. I'm simply programming my mental computer. I order my brain to release youth-giving hormones and chemicals into my body.

On entering the dining room just after my speech, I overheard two women discussing the food at the buffet table. One said, "All I have to do is look at food, and I gain ten pounds." The other woman said, "I can eat whatever I want and never gain a pound." I wondered if each of these women had just, intentionally or unintentionally, programmed her body's computer. Were their brains just following orders? It is indeed food for thought.

My husband has never gone to bed due to an illness. In 50 years, he has never had the flu, he has never had a severe cold; basically, he has never been sick! He has had one elective surgery and recovered more quickly than the doctor expected. I know you might find this hard to believe—a man in his 70s who has never suffered from illness of any kind—but it is true. Shortly after we married, if health was the topic of conversation, he would reply, "I never get sick, I never get sick." His mother and father both died in their early 60s. Looking back, the longevity gene is not apparent, yet my husband can work circles around other men his age.

So, are we slaves to our genes, or can we actually influence how fast (or slowly) and how well we will age? Can we slow down the aging factor? I believe the answer is yes, there are many things we can do. To look 40 at 55 without surgery is doable, but you need to program your body's computer.

When it comes to beating the aging clock, use the power of the brain and develop the art of visual imaging. Sit back, relax, close your eyes, and visualize yourself ten to twenty years from today. Visualize the woman you wish to become—how you will look, what you will weigh, your secret self, and the lifestyle you desire. The effects of visualization, using the power of your mind, are incredible.

What you visualize is the programming system for your subconscious mind. Once you have developed a clear picture in your mind, your subconscious mind fires up and responds, attempting to formulate a plan to make the pictures a reality.

At the age of 16, I began to visualize myself traveling around the world speaking to thousands of people. It took 25 years, but my dream came true. In the following 20 years, I have covered more than three million air miles. It took 25 years, but when the time was right, my vision became my reality. Trust me—visualization works. I am a firm believer in the power of the mind to trigger your subconscious to make that which you visualize a reality.

If you picture yourself 30 pounds overweight at 60, you will achieve that preconceived visual image. If you took Heidi Klum's head and transplanted it onto Rosie O'Donnell's body, how long would it take before Rosie's body would begin a miraculous change? From day one, change would begin—because the body would have a new computer (or brain) giving instructions.

To experience the power of visual imaging use this little experiment. Close your eyes, visualize yourself in your kitchen facing the refrigerator, opening the refrigerator door. Be sure you keep your eyes closed and visualize a big, juicy lemon. Pick it up and smell it. Now take the lemon over to the counter, get a knife, and cut it open. Visualize the juice running over the counter. Eyes closed, put your head back, and squirt some of the sour juice into your mouth. If this doesn't get your saliva juices flowing, you need better visualization skills. This is a great way to prove the brain's reaction to our thoughts. Your thoughts are the input you use to throw the anti-aging switch. Your brain controls every part of your body, so feed it well and program it aggressively.

The second most influential body organ that holds a key to anti-aging is the human heart. The most powerful anti-aging emotion that exists is in the human heart.

I once asked a man I had never met personally to invest two million dollars in one of my companies. I ended my phone call by asking him to listen to his heart's voice. Two days later, he phoned and said, "My head says no, but my heart says yes."

In matters of love, most people listen to their heart's voice over their head's voice. As you learn to listen to your heart, you will hear a message urging you to love one another. (LOVE is discussed in a later chapter.)

Stressed Out Does Not Make a Beauty Queen

If you are a fan of the TV show The Biggest Loser, *then you have watched the shock on the faces of people who have just been told their internal age compared with their actual age. Everyone has a birthday each year, but your chronological age has little to do with your body's health age.

Your health age will be determined by your lifestyle and the choices you make:

* the amount of exercise you have committed to daily
* the food choices that feed every inch of your body
* your alcohol consumption (or lack thereof)
* the amount of sleep you are committed to every night
* your physical and emotional stress levels, and your ability to manage both (emotional stress produces physical stress, and *stress is the greatest cause of overall aging*)

My seatmate on a cross-country flight intrigued me. He had the look of an extremely studious professional student. As I enjoy exploring the minds of super-intellects, I began a conversation with this man. After the usual plane chitchat, I asked him about his life. He went on to tell me he had spent many years as a traveling companion of Albert Einstein. I asked him what he felt was the most important lesson on life he had learned from Mr. Einstein. He said Mr. Einstein had told him to listen to that still, small voice in his head.

At that moment, that man confirmed my belief. That voice, or your subconscious mind, is trying to help you solve your problems. The subconscious mind is a marvelous power, a force working at all times to lift you to new heights of peace, health, and happiness.

I believe this may be one of the methods God uses to guide us to the abundant life he desires for us. But most people in the world use their free will to override that still, small voice. The voice says, "Don't eat that," but we eat it anyway. The next day we step on our scales for our daily weigh-in and suffer the consequences of our decision. The voice says, "Keep the information you just heard to yourself," but this is really juicy gossip, so we fight the voice.

I sincerely believe our bodies, via our brains, talk to us all the time, but most people refuse to listen, and as a result get sick from stress. Your body warns you it is tired and needs rest, but you override the message, telling yourself the party sounds like so much fun you just have to go. Your body clearly sends a sign you are working too many hours. You override the voice by thinking you can't afford to work fewer hours as you need the money. The voice says this job is stressing you out, so "Quit," but you ignore the voice by reasoning it is too hard to find a new job. So you stay, and hate the eight hours you are there.

The voice may hold in its power your health and just how fast you will age, or how long you will live. Each time you override the voice, stress hormones and chemicals rush through your body. Toxic hormones affect every organ in your body, including your skin—your body's largest organ.

I made my connection between health, aging, and stress more than 35 years ago when my mother was diagnosed with lymphoma (cancer). My parents owned and operated clothing stores. My father worked as a stock-broker. My mother managed the stores but was not a business woman by nature. Her true talent was that of a mom and volunteer. She was also an exceptional seamstress and cook, and her leadership skills were used well at the church. All these things she loved.

At first, she had fun managing the clothing store but as the business grew, the fun turned into overwhelming stress for her. One store was held up at gunpoint several times. Every day she would get out of bed and say to herself, "I don't want to do this anymore; I do not want to do this another day." Mom wanted out! But being a good wife, she acceded to my father's desire that she wait until she was 65. Every day she would override her feelings and the voice, put on a happy face, and go to work. Her body and soul needed rest, but she refused to listen.

The first sign of trouble came when her blood pressure rose to 200. It is a wonder she lived, but after a short hospital stay, she found herself back in the store. Thinking of herself as a responsible person, she could not say no to my father. One sure way to relieve the body of stress is by dying. In a short time, cancer spread throughout her body. We were told she might not have long to live. My father responded to the diagnosis by putting their two stores up for sale. Immediately her body was relieved of the stress affecting her life and health.

My mother, who the doctors said 40 years ago did not have long to live, lived to celebrate her 75th wedding anniversary. I believe her subconscious mind supported her decision when she rejected her doctor's medical suggestions and took a spiritual path to healing. Every day was not just a focus on body healing—every day was centered on mind, body, and soul healing. And with the stress of owning the stores gone, the healing began. She was once again her true, natural self. Her soul was filled with joy.

Her favorite song throughout her healing was,

Because He Lives I can face tomorrow.
Because He lives all fear is gone.
Because I know He holds the future,
Life is worth the living just because He lives.

She sang it repeatedly, my mother, a beautiful woman at 93. It was almost magical. Once she was out from under the stress that had plagued her for so long, she began to pray and heal and heal and pray. She focused on her spiritual life and her nutritional intake by eating biblically. She rested, and she survived. God blessed her life. Not all people will take the path she chose and perhaps not all people should, but in her case, it worked. My mother died, still beautiful, at age 94.

I, too, found myself in a stressful job situation in 1977 working for the Walt Disney Company. All my actions were minutely monitored as I was hired to solve a problem created by my boss. His future depended on my success in solving and correcting a mistake of his making. Talk about stress! Before the year's end, I too had cancer.

In some families stress and tension may turn into cancer, arthritis, stomach ulcers, alcoholism, or diabetes. One never knows for sure, but *one* thing is for sure—negative stress will affect your body's aging and health, somehow, some way. When both my mother and I developed cancer during a five-year period, I went looking for answers. We had eaten right, did not abuse our bodies, lived a healthy lifestyle, and cancer had never been a part of our family's medical history. The only negative factor we both had was stress. I left Disney and went to work achieving all my lifetime dreams and goals. For me, surgery was the answer, but each person must decide what is right for her.

Few people live stress-free; in fact, it is an unrealistic goal. To be alive means that you will know stress. No one is immune to stress, but some people appear to handle it better than others.

The second life-changing idea told me by Albert Einstein's companion: Always be a child. Never lose the excitement, the joy of life, found in investigating and being inquisitive about all things. Never lose that spirit that lives in a child's heart. Learn to love the simple pleasures of life. Take time to examine a spider's web or a hummingbird's nest. Take pleasure in warm sand or a melting Popsicle. Play with your friends and laugh a lot.

Some say stress brings out the best in us, while others say we are killing ourselves and must stress-proof our lives. But no one is immune. If you want to test your stress temperament, I suggest you drive the Los Angeles freeways during rush hour. If you can breeze through that for a few weeks, I would say you will make it through your child's terrible twos and teenage years. Indeed some women appear to handle stress with few signs of pressure. These same women appear to ward off those premature facial lines we hate. Where is the Botox? Research indicates that these women share personality traits in common: faith in God, faith in themselves, a high level of self-esteem, self-confidence, a positive attitude, control of their self-image through diet, exercise, and personal pride, and their willingness to accept challenge.

Stress is one of the formidable problems we face in our modern society, despite all the creature comforts we enjoy. We drive SUVs with built-in entertainment systems. We have all forms of convenience foods to pack in the kids' lunch-boxes. We have machines that wash and dry our clothes and dishes. With a click of a computer mouse, we can access information on any topic, once only available at our local library, if there. We have packaged dinners ready at the push of a microwave button. We have clothes fabrics that do not require ironing. We can exercise with an iPod in our ear and a cell phone in our pocket, keeping us forever in touch with our kingdom. And yet, we are the most stressed generation in history.

The United States of America has 6 percent of the world's population, yet we take 90 percent of the anxiety drugs. Why? What's wrong with us? One friend confessed to me how much happier she was when she had less. She told me she and her husband were stressed beyond reason just managing all the money they made. She moved to Colorado, now raises bees, and she's no longer stressed.

What's wrong with us? There was a time in history when people sat on porches and talked to each other. Today, we fight over the remote control and allow someone on the television to do all the talking. It is not just adults who are stressed, our children are stressed. With schedules so packed, they eat many meals in the car going from music lessons to soccer practice. *Busy* has become a power word.

As the grandmother of six, I can confirm we are passing on our over-filled lives to our children. We are losing the battle. We no longer know how to just rest, to rest quietly, and just turn off and tune out the world. Are we wound up so tightly we can no longer define the word *relax*? Mothers say, "Relax"—what does that mean? Well, I will remind you. It means no work or responsibility for an allotted interval of time—time for you to unwind, stretch out, and take it easy. Being a woman who has raised two children, but has also spent years in the professional world, I know that raising children is by far the hardest job in the entire world, despite what some people think.

Learn to take time for yourself without feeling guilty. I once thought it wrong to just relax. I had to teach myself that resting did not indicate I was lazy. Giving yourself permission to rest your mind, body, and soul will go a long way in your efforts to slow down the aging clock. Stress accomplishes nothing but poor health, sleeplessness, and increased lines on your face. If you want to look fabulous at 40 and unforgettable at 50, check your stress levels—live with God at the wheel as you speed through life. Turn to God, lay that stress at his feet, and age will come more gracefully.

But leaving your stress at God's feet is not always easy. It takes practice to develop the level of faith required to completely give your life and the lives of your family over to an unseen God—but that is what believing is all about. As your faith increases, your stress level decreases. Faith is the confident assurance something we want to happen is going to happen. It is the certainty what we hope for is waiting for us, even though we cannot see it; faith is *believing*.

You are the one, the only one, who can run your life the way you know is best for you. Never give control of your life over to another human being. No one can tell you what is best for you, only you know that. Life grinds us down. Our spine compresses and after a day's work, we are three-quarters of an inch shorter. Stress makes you say, "Somehow, some way, my life is out of control." Research concludes 25 percent of the population is chronically stressed.

A woman walked into my "It's About You" office, and as she began to tell me her story, it was evident she was under tremendous stress. She had worked without a break for twenty years straight. The only break from her work was to give birth to her beloved little girl. Anyone who has ever had a baby knows you get no sleep the first eight weeks of that baby's life! She returned to work after eight weeks and still, five years later, has had little rest. I fear she is heading toward a lifestyle train wreck.

America needs to take a lesson from Europe, where, on occasion, workers get three months away from the job. If you want to de-stress (*and* de-age), walk, exercise, sleep, eat healthy foods, and once again give your problems, cares, and worries over to the Master Healer. God says, "Be still, and know that I am God!" (Psalm 46:10 NIV). Turn off the TV, close the computer, hide the I-pod, shut down the cell phone, turn the kids over to Grandma, send your husband out to play golf, and just spend some time alone.

Synonyms for Stress

Intensity, pressure, burden, hardship, over-exertion, agony, affliction, anxiety, nervousness, fearfulness, apprehensiveness, impatience, fear, agitation, tension, passion, frustration, restlessness, misgiving, mistrust, alarm, dread, trembling, urgency, jitters, unrest, strain, apprehension.

WHO NEEDS IT?

As stress is so destructive to your physical, mental, and emotional health, you will find I have addressed elements of stress throughout *Anti-Aging God's Way*.

Letting Go

Read this over. Study it. Pray over it and you will find letting go of your load will release a peace within you that will allow your spirit to soar free, let you completely give your burdens to God . . . and let the work be done within you where the need is anyway.

> To let go doesn't mean to stop caring; it means I can't do it for someone else.
> To let go is not to cut myself off; it's the realization I can't control another.
> To let go is not to enable, but to allow learning from natural consequences.
> To let go is to admit powerlessness, which means the outcome is not in my hands.
> To let go is not to change or blame another; I can only change myself.
> To let go is not to care *for,* but to care *about.*
> To let go is not to fix, but to be supportive.
> To let go is not to judge, but to allow another to be a human being.
> To let go is not to be in the middle arranging outcomes, but to allow others to affect their own outcomes.
> To let go is not to be unprotective, it is to permit another to face reality.

To let go is not to deny, but to accept.

To let go is not to nag, scold, or argue, but to search out my own
   shortcomings and correct them.

To let go is not to adjust everything to my desires, but to take each
   day as it comes and to cherish the moment.

To let go is not to criticize anyone, but to try to become what I dream
   I can be.

To let go is not to regret the past, but to grow and live for the future.

To let go is to fear less and love more.

To let go, and to let God, is to find peace!

—AUTHOR UNKNOWN

Kay's Mistake

Kay, a woman I knew for more than 16 years, died last year. Kay was a
lovely woman about 60 who worked in my building. Visiting one day, she
shared with me some female difficulties she had been having. I pleaded
with her to see a doctor. Kay also shared with me the stress she was under
caring for her elderly parents. She finally did see a doctor but never came
home again. In six short weeks, Kay aged twenty years as the last stages of
cancer took her life.

This had been her routine at the time of our conversation: After a full
week's work, she would drive 50 miles to her parents' home to cook a full
week's worth of meals. I asked her why she was doing this when her brother
lived close to his parents. She said her parents didn't want anyone else to
do it. I asked her why she was doing this when her parents could afford an
outside service. After a little digging, it came to light that her brother was
the chosen child in the family. After all these years, Kay was still trying to
gain her parents' approval.

I advised Kay that since her parents were in their 80s, they were not
going to change. "Tell them," I suggested, "that you are exhausted and
stressed beyond belief." She was so worried how her parents might react if
she was honest and said, "I can't do this anymore."

I believe it killed her. Seeking human approval is a waste of your time. Instead, concentrate on seeking *God's* approval.

"Refuse to Be Discouraged"

If you are feeling stressed, read the following poem just before bed:

I refuse to be discouraged. To be sad, or to cry;
I refuse to be downhearted, and here's the reason why:
I have a God who's mighty, who's sovereign and supreme;
I have a God who loves me, and I am on his team.
He is all-wise and powerful, Jehovah is his name;
Though everything is changeable, my God remains the same.
My God knows all that's happening, beginning to the end;
His presence is my comfort; he is my dearest friend.
When sickness comes to weaken me, to bring my head down low,
I call upon my mighty God; into his arms I go.
When circumstances threaten to rob me of my peace,
He draws me close unto his breast, where all my strivings cease.
When my heart melts within me, and weakness takes control,
He gathers me into his arms, he soothes my heart and soul.
The great "I Am" is with me, my life is in his hand;
The "God of Jacob" is my hope; it's in his strength I stand.
I refuse to be defeated, my eyes are on my God;
He promised to be with me as through my life I trod.
I'm looking past all my circumstances to Heaven's throne above;
My prayers have reached the Heart of God, I'm resting in his love.
I give God thanks in everything, my eyes are on his face;
The battle's his, the victory mine; he'll help me win the race.

—Lita Kurtzer

Your attitude and thoughts are working every minute on the condition of your face twenty-five years from today. The pace and pressures of your life may be keeping you exhausted, and exhaustion shows on the face first. If your friends tell you that you look tired, you probably are. Strive for a relaxed, tension-free face.

A new study shows that stress hormones produce brain lesions, which may speed up the progression of Alzheimer's disease. Break the rules of personal and emotional health, and stress will eventually break you. Many factors influence the pace at which we age. Emotions play as big a part as physical illness or sun damage. The stability or instability of your emotional life affects every muscle in your body. One path to health is in your ability to eliminate stress by making solid, competent, virtuous decisions. The world's way says, "Stressed out? Take this mood-altering drug and make an appointment with your therapist." God's Way says, "Turn your life over to me. 'I am the Alpha and the Omega—the beginning and the end' (Revelation 1:8 NLT). I hold the universe in my hands."

Leaving Your Worries on God's Doorstep

Are those worry lines on your face getting deeper? Do you really want a younger face? There is a wonderful old hymn:

> *Trust and obey,*
> *For there's no other way*
> *To be happy in Jesus*
> *But to trust and obey.*

How much better our lives would be and how many worry lines could we lose if we would just do what the song says—trust and obey.

If you just trusted, really trusted, wouldn't you find life easier, and your face more relaxed and beautiful? But trusting takes faith. Do you have enough faith to turn your worries, cares, and problems over to the Lord? We go to church and give our worries to God, then we take them back again before the end of the day. Give them up, and do not take them back. Why are we so arrogant as to think we can do a better job than the Lord, the Master of the Universe, at solving problems?

Needless worry will add years to your face and accomplish nothing but poor health and sleepless nights. Worry saps your energy pointlessly. If you spend time worrying about your tomorrows, you may realize too late you missed your todays. Worry will age you as quickly as the sun turns a plum into a prune. If you practice living one day at a time and fully trust in God, worry will not become an aging factor for you. Leave your worries on God's doorstep. Worry is such a waste of time—since it accomplishes nothing. Worry is showing very little confidence in God's love for you.

Lean on him. Any problems or worry you face can be handled with God's help. Depend on God for strength on any problem you are facing. It could be as simple as an addiction to chocolate chip cookies or hot fudge sundaes that worries you and causes you to hate how you look. But he knows and is there to help. Worry and stress can cause gastrointestinal disturbances, acid reflux disease, and irritable bowel syndrome, according to a study presented at the American College of Gastroenterology and reported in the *Albany Times Union.*

> *Yet the Lord still waits for you to come to him, so he can show*
> *you his love, he will conquer you to bless you, just as he said.*
> *For the Lord is faithful to his promises. Blessed are all*
> *those who wait for him to help them.*
>
> —ISAIAH 30:18

In Matthew 6:25, Jesus said, *"Therefore I tell you, do not worry about your life,"* and in Mathew 6:34 we read, *"Therefore do not worry about tomorrow, for tomorrow will worry about itself"* (NIV).

My objective is to help you understand the 75/25 percent formula (75 percent internal, 25 percent external). How you think and what you believe can make the difference in your appearance twenty-five years from today. "Beauty is only skin deep" is indeed a fact. For long-term beauty, guard the inside with the same dedication you give the outside.

Oh, put God to the test and see how kind he is! See for yourself
the way his mercies shower down on all who trust him.
—PSALM 34:8

Rest in the Lord; wait patiently for him to act.
—PSALM 37:7

I am leaving you with a gift—peace of mind and heart! And the
peace I give isn't fragile like the peace the world gives.
So don't be troubled or afraid.
—JOHN 14:27

I have told you all this so that you will
have peace of heart and mind.
—JOHN 16:33

Don't worry about anything.
—PHILIPPIANS 4:6

The Bible tells us if we will commit to this lifestyle we will have peace, and peace is a beautiful thing.

The Liability of Guilt and the Healing Beauty of Forgiveness

Few words in the thesaurus have the ability to annihilate the mind, body, and soul as does the word *guilt*. Little devastates your health, your heart, your mind, your soul, and your face more than guilt. It's a common practice to have a minister or priest visit a dying prisoner in hopes he can leave the earth a little less burdened by guilt. My own children tell me the best advice I ever passed on to them was to "lead a guilt-free life."

Years ago, I was speaking to a gathering of medical doctors and health care specialists. After the question-and-answer period, I asked them if *I* could ask a question. My question was simply, "Can you tell me why there are so many sick people? Most people in your hospitals are not there due to an accident, but your hospitals are full." They answered, "Their insides are eating them up!" I then asked, "What eats up people's insides?" The reply: "Emotions." The doctors believed that 85 percent of all hospitalizations were not due to physical problems alone but due to emotional problems that had manifested themselves in a physical illness.

I then asked, "What emotion is the cause of so much illness?" Their answer? "Guilt." Guilt is the most destructive emotion one can have. People think, 'Why did I / why didn't I?' 'I should have / I shouldn't have.' 'Will someone find out?' If guilt eats us up and brings on the premature aging of our bodies, we must find a way to avoid the deterioration and destruction it causes. Of all the emotions that affect your body in a toxic manner, few are more destructive than guilt.

Many have found the answer—cleansing their soul by leaving their guilt at Jesus' feet. Jesus came for just that reason. He took all our shame and guilt on himself; he gave us a way to become free and gave us a new start. I have heard people say upon walking away from the Cross, how much lighter they felt! After all, guilt is a heavy load that can weigh you down. Let us keep our goal in mind. Our goal is to save our health and face using common sense and a life grounded on good decision making. It takes maturity to determine what is right or wrong for your life, yet mature, well-educated people consistently make self-destructive, guilt-ridden decisions.

After heeding the doctors' words, I made the decision to develop a lifetime philosophy to lead a guilt-free life. That philosophy led to life changes. I analyzed each of my personal relationships. I asked myself if I needed to deal with any guilt feelings in regard to the condition of any relationships. Was there forgiveness and/or love needed? At times, pride would raise its ugly head, but in time, the words "I am sorry" or "Forgive me" became easier to say.

The road to greater happiness is paved with stepping stones of kindness. If you are a giving person, you may have this virtue down pat. Your kindness to others is not the issue. Do you know how to be kind to yourself? Do you give generously to others but suffer from feelings of guilt when you indulge yourself? There is a time to give, but there is also a time to receive. The Bible notes that Jesus once said, "It is more blessed to give than to receive" (Acts 20:35 NIV) but that only establishes a priority. It does not eliminate the need to receive.

It may seem bizarre, but there does come a time when a new fishing pole for Dad or a new outfit for Mom is more important than new bicycles for the kids. The willingness to sacrifice all joy and pleasure in your life for the sake of another person simply does not make sense. You must learn to find a balance between your needs and those of others.

There are parents who sacrifice every vacation, every weekend trip, and all forms of entertainment just to keep their children clothed in the latest fashions or tucked away in a prestigious school. Image and education can be loving gifts, but if they come at the expense of the parents' marital happiness or their own sense of well-being, someone will have to pay the cost: a damaged self, a fragile marriage, a selfish child. Is guilt somehow involved here?

Consideration for the welfare of others makes you a gracious, thoughtful person. But do not become a martyr to others' happiness, or you will also be a recipient of their pity. Common-sense consideration for your wants, welfare, and needs translates into higher self-esteem and more energy to help others. The world is full of takers, people who are ready and willing to abuse the giving nature of others. Do not let yourself be abused in this way.

People unable to show kindness to themselves often become old, miserable, bitter people. Suffering becomes their lifestyle, self-pity their reward. A good rule to remember: Every day do or say something to brighten the lives of those around you. Then, to be truly content and happy, also do something kind for yourself.

Marcia, in her mid-30s, prefers men many years her junior. She becomes intimately involved with one man after another. She is a graduate of one of America's most prestigious universities and is highly intelligent. However, her decision-making processes are driven by low self-worth, lack of self-confidence, and little or no self-control. As a result, she suffers from anger, frustration, and guilt due to her bad decisions. Bonnie Raitt sings a song that says, "Your history shows all over your face." If Marcia remains on this path, her history will be all over her pretty face sooner rather than later.

Guilt is the result of actions or events experienced during our life that cause us to feel blame or shame. Holding on to guilt will cause serious health consequences. If the guilt is of a magnitude such that it causes you endless hours of worry or lack of sleep, health problems will develop from the stress. Stress causes medical problems and illnesses such as stomachaches, digestive disorders, depression, anxiety, headaches, and wrinkles. The longer you hold on to the guilt, the more your face will reflect the stress. Take those guilt feelings to God. Free your mind, soul, and face of guilt. We must live our lives with no regrets. God can free you from your past and guide you toward a new beginning.

What happiness for those whose guilt has been forgiven! What joys when sins are covered over! What relief for those who have confessed their sins and God has cleared their record.

—PSALM 32:1–2

Take the Test of Time

Take a long-stem glass and a pile of stones. Hold the glass at arm's length in front of you, and then put one stone in the glass for every negative, destructive, and guilt-laden emotion you are holding onto. There could be one stone for anger, one for bitterness, one for envy, one for hatred, one for worry, and a big stone for guilt and sins. Don't let your arm rest. Continue to hold it out, and keep putting stones into the glass until you have completed your list of destructive feelings or emotions. These include feelings toward those who have hurt you, as well as guilt and negative feelings you hold inside about yourself. As you put each stone in your glass, time is not on your side. Just how long can you hold the glass out in front of you before your arm begins to hurt? Keep holding and soon your arm is weak. Continue holding on, and eventually, your arm's tension and fatigue will spread to your whole body.

Many women have sat in my office with tears running down their cheeks, desperately looking for affirmation that they are special and worthy. Dawn took two hours to tell me of mental and physical abuse at the hands of her father. She was holding a big emotional glass filled with stones of hatred, bitterness, and contempt. Illness was heading her way. The rocks were doing their job. One day, Dawn will find herself in a hospital being tested for some mysterious illness. Perhaps the emotional rocks in your life have already taken root as serious headaches or fibromyalgia, heart or muscle pain, lack of sleep, or some disease you can do little about.

Anxious as we are to slow the aging process, a step in the right direction is to call on God to rid your soul of any guilt or bitterness you are harboring. Remember—every second of your life, chemicals and hormones are coursing through your veins. With every emotion, those chemicals and hormones are working for, or against, your physical well-being. There is a chemical mixture for "I'm ignorant," as well as a mixture for "I'm an intelligent person." There is a mixture for "Why me?" as well as a mixture for "Why not me?" And one for "Will God ever forgive me?" Yes, he will, but you must confess your transgressions to him, and then ask for forgiveness.

Your brain can only work in accordance with the programming it receives from you, and the programming it receives drives the circuit board that sends out the messages to all your cells.

Why is guilt so difficult to disengage from our life? First, no human has the power to pardon sins, and second, human nature makes it hard to admit we were wrong. Many find it hard to say "I apologize," "I made a mistake," or "I messed up." There are many ways to say I'm sorry. Why are we neglectful at doing so? We are indeed a forgiving country; it is in our culture.

The power of giving and receiving forgiveness is immeasurable. It takes wisdom to know what is important, and exoneration is important. In those times when an act has been perpetrated on us so great we feel unable to forgive, we must release it to God and allow him to deal with the offender in his way. The act of releasing the frustration, the anger, the hostility, and the rage to God is powerfully healing.

Forgiving is not the same as condoning. It never makes right what has been done to you. Forgiveness sets you free. You cut the strings, and you release the hold you have on the other person's throat.

I was once deeply hurt by a couple of people in my church. The pain was so deep I had little sleep for days. The accusations were totally untrue. I gave it over to God and in a short period of time, he allowed the truth to come to light. The peace of knowing that an all-powerful God can take my hurt, comfort me, and then shine light on the truth is priceless. No cream for sale on the face of the earth can give you peace and mend a broken heart. Meeting God personally will flood your body with the best anti-aging medicine the world has to offer. It's the miracle of peace that surpasses all understanding. Jesus gave his life for us. Yet it seems so very hard for us to mutter a few words of forgiveness, even though we claim to be a follower of the teachings of the Bible. If we are truly committed to the ways of Christ, one of the very first acts we acknowledge is Christ's forgiveness of our transgressions. Why then can't we forgive? True forgiveness must come from the heart.

Treat others as you
want them to treat you.
—LUKE 6:31

This, the Golden Rule, is the teaching of the laws of Moses in a nutshell.

Not forgiving someone, with or without accompanying guilt, will bring you deep sorrow. When you hurt, your face will reflect the pain. Forgive, and then allow God to deal with the person who gave you the pain. We've all had someone cause us emotional pain, but we have all caused someone else emotional pain as well.

Emotional pain, one pain we all have in common, is a significant factor in aging. Where we take our pain and how we respond to emotional pain is one important part of *Anti-Aging God's Way*. You can internalize your pain, but eventually, emotional pain will surface, hitting your heart and eventually your face. It never stays inside you. Pain comes out through anger or emotional turmoil. Forgiving is a choice, never a feeling. You choose to forgive the offender and the offense. Building trust is another issue and may take more time than simply giving the gift of forgiveness.

How do we make it through the ups and downs of life on our own, without God to help us? After we have exhausted all our resources and still can't solve our deepest problems and pain, we finally decide there must be a God who is willing to listen. Without God, where do we go with the hurt, anger, grief, and turmoil that life brings? Every emotion expressed with the muscles of your face affects every muscle of your body.

Of all the myriad emotions that affect your body in a positive or negative manner, few are more powerful than guilt. Your body's emotional response to guilt is overwhelmingly adverse. Repugnant emotions attack your healthy immune system and contaminate your organs, making you vulnerable to illness and premature aging. The more negative your thoughts, the more damage to your cells, the more lines on your face. The more positive your thoughts, the healthier your cells, the fewer lines on your face. The essence of youthful skin no matter your age is your goal. So forgive, forgive, and forgive; first yourself, then those who caused you suffering.

To understand successful aging, one must first understand that guilt is the effect of bad decision making. One of my clients is in the middle of a bad divorce. Her 54-year-old husband decided to move in with his twenty-nine-year-old assistant. His actions have resulted in his losing complete control of his life. His vindictiveness and guilt have aged him twenty years in two years, and his health is being affected on a grand scale. He continues to compound bad decision on top of bad decision, which is now being reflected in the decisions his teenage children are making.

Very few things eat away at our health, hearts, minds, souls, and faces as does guilt. Guilt is so pervasive and destructive to a happy life that there is a much-visited website where people can go to unburden their guilt and ask for forgiveness. *After much investigation, the life philosophy I chose for myself is to lead a guilt-free life to the best of my ability.*

To be guilt-free one must consider the power of forgiveness. As I mentioned in the preface to *Anti-Aging God's Way,* someone hurt me to the core of my very soul. As this person lay dying, I knew I had but one choice and that was to forgive. Clinging to resentment is like taking poison and then waiting for the other person to die.

As a Christian, I know I have been forgiven, therefore my intellect and soul direct me to forgive. My father could no longer speak, but he could hear. I told him he had hurt me deeply but I forgave him. He squeezed my hand tightly and died that night. Both of us were now free—me from hurt, resentment, and the feeling of betrayal; my father from a world filled with suffering, grief, and embittered souls.

Doctors have long suspected, and with today's modern technology have confirmed, that people who don't forgive tend to be sick. Often physical illness directly results from an unforgiving spirit. Our bodies are not designed to bear the burden of bitterness and anger; in the long run, they break down one way or another under the stress and strain. This doesn't mean that everyone who is sick needs to forgive someone; it does, however, mean that long-term refusal to forgive can cause physical afflictions.

Are you suffering from stomach trouble, heart palpitations, or inability to sleep? Is it possible these symptoms ultimately come from an unforgiving heart rather than strictly from physical causes? Could that unforgiving heart be the torturer? Ask the Lord to give you some answers.

If we refuse to let go of the pain of injustice, or if we strive to get even, we put ourselves in an emotional prison, the worst kind of captivity. But when we extend mercy and forgiveness, sharing with others what God has shared with us, we enjoy glorious freedom.

— Kay Arthur, David & BJ Lawson
Forgiveness: Breaking the Power of the Past

Forgiveness:

- ❊ Is an act of the will.
- ❊ Is cleansing.
- ❊ Releases your trapped spirit.
- ❊ Will eliminate toxic emotions.

Jesus died to forgive us. All it takes for us to forgive is the willingness of our heart.

The Dangers of Denial

Are you in a state of denial concerning something in your life? Recently I received a call from a business partner who confessed to me he had just realized he was obsessed with golf and that his obsession was affecting his life, including his marriage. Today I read a story of a 5'9" man who weighed 360 pounds and did not consider himself fat. That is denial at or near its worst. Right now look at your circumstances. What are you possibly in denial of?

A bad relationship
Your work schedule
Your lifestyle
Your health
Your weight
Your relationship with God
Your financial situation
Your marriage
Your parental responsibilities
Your mortality
Your ability to love unconditionally
The fact that smoking will give *you* lung cancer
Your belief that you can actually change your spouse
Your belief that you can lose weight by diet alone
The need for saying the words "I love you"

If we are balanced, each area of life will receive attention and nurturing. Life balance plays a major role in your ability to age gracefully, elegantly, healthily, slowly. The human body is a machine and, like any machine, must be balanced and cared for with proper timing to run smoothly. To ride a bicycle, you must learn to balance. For a plane to get off the ground, it must be balanced. Perhaps you are badly out of balance and in denial of the damage you are doing to your body. If that is the case, it may take a health crash to get your attention.

I confess I learned balance the hard way. From the age of 16, my dream was to become a professional speaker. I practiced my art as my daughters grew up. Once they were raised, I knew it was time to fulfill my dream. I jumped on the whirlwind ride of professional speaking. With my husband's blessings, I started to travel. My dream was coming true; I was on tour with many of the most famous names in the industry. Up to eight flights a month: London, Sydney, Rio, Auckland, Hong Kong, you name it, and I was making money beyond my dreams and truly having a great time.

Little by little my health began to show signs of wear and tear from constant travel. I was extremely out of balance but completely unaware, until I ended up in the hospital with a very serious problem. I was on such a high I still did not realize, lying in my hospital bed, that I was in trouble. Finally a doctor told me I was in denial. My question: denial of what? Just like many overachievers, I did not understand. All my friends and promoters heard I was in the hospital, and I received a roomful of flowers. My attitude was that of a partygoer, as I did not feel sick, even though I was not allowed to get out of bed. After twelve days, I was sent home with strict rules to follow.

Two weeks later, I received a phone call from one of my doctor's partners checking on my medication. He was trying to remember who I was, so I described myself to him. All of a sudden he said, "Oh, I remember—you are the one who was so sick." At that moment, the light went on. I am not sure, to this day, if it was denial or medical ignorance. A blood clot had broken off and traveled to my lungs. Perhaps not understanding the severity of my condition was a blessing, as I was very optimistic. The thought of death never entered my mind.

Is your body being poisoned due to your lifestyle? Are you feeling exhausted for no reason? Do you yell? Are you irritable, impatient, screaming, hard to please? Out-of-balance women often find it difficult to meet the physical needs of their husbands. Attempting to be the perfect wife, mother, hostess, employee, friend, and daughter, and at the same time strive for the perfect body, face, and lifestyle is striving for the impossible. If that describes you, you are out of balance, and unbalance is one major cause of illness.

After I realized I, indeed, was out of balance and my health was being seriously affected, I came to my senses. No amount of money is worth as much as your health. It took a serious jolt to get my attention.

Hopefully you understand the value of balancing and de-stressing your life. In doing so, you are heading toward a more productive life. However if you are still so stressed that it is making you depressed, there is still work to be done. Depression and a beautiful, serene face are not compatible— or what God intended. Feeling dejected, downhearted, and sad is no way to live. When women come to me with those symptoms, one of the first areas I address with them is whether they are leading a balanced lifestyle. Today, one in five people is chemically depressed. That is ten times more than twenty years ago. What are we doing to ourselves? How do we help ourselves?

Guidelines for Good Decision Making

As a result of my philosophy and my health issues, I sat down and wrote a set of guidelines to help me in the decision-making process:

* Is the decision I am about to make constructive or destructive?
* Will this decision lead me toward long-term happiness or short-term pleasure? (Dieters take note.)
* Will this decision benefit my family?
* Will this decision leave me guilt-free?
* Is this decision good for my health?
* Am I making an unreasonable demand on myself?
* Am I living up to my potential?
* Am I driven by fear?
* Is this decision consistent with my standards and philosophies?
* Will this decision lend itself to God's primary purpose for my life?

* Does this decision make sense?
* What are my ultimate goals and motives in making this decision?
* Is this decision God-centered—or me-centered?

Copy this list and use it to help you establish decision-making guidelines for yourself. In our lifetime, we make a limited number of major life decisions. But most of the decisions that guide our lives are relatively small. Those small decisions, by the thousands, come together like little drops of rain to form a beautiful waterfall or a destructive flood. One little drop of water at a time, one little decision at a time. Flood or waterfall, you are the master of your kingdom. You are the product of your life decisions for good or for bad. It takes wisdom to make quality decisions, and it takes even greater wisdom and courage to forgive and ask for forgiveness. The act of releasing your frustration, your anger, your hostility, and your rage is extremely healing, especially for the muscles of your face.

You—Wonderful Beyond Imagination

This is Mary's story. Some people age in accordance with their self-worth, self-image, and confidence levels. I learned this lesson in my middle twenties after opening my first business. At that time, I believed aging, or the appearance of age, was simply an outside condition, one that manifested itself totally in the way a woman wore her clothes, her hair, and her makeup, and cared for her skin. By just restyling the woman, I could make her appear younger. Little did I realize at that tender age, there was much more to beauty than new makeup and beautiful clothes.

The day Mary walked into my studio and inquired about classes I was very excited. My youthful exuberance took over because I knew I could help this dowdy-appearing woman look fabulous. She was in her 30s but looked like a woman of 50. She had allowed herself and her appearance to wane greatly: a good twenty-five pounds overweight, hair too short, and very little makeup. I did not see her as she was; I saw her as I knew she could be—a real standout. I believed that by the time she finished my self-improvement course she would be my walking, breathing advertisement.

I went to work on her diet-and-exercise plan. I advised her to grow her hair and taught her all about makeup, fashion, and style. The day came for her graduation. I instructed her on what to wear on her newly streamlined body, had her hair styled to my guidelines, and applied her makeup. Once we completed the transition from dowdy and middle-aged to fabulous beauty, I stood back and considered myself a genius!

At that point, I was sure women would beat a path to my studio. I sent Mary home to her husband and immediately received a phone call of gratitude. Men are visual creatures, so her husband was thrilled. Mary looked beautiful, for what I believe was the first time in her adult life. I did not see Mary again for six months. Visiting a new church and standing in the vestibule, I saw a woman who looked vaguely familiar. As she came closer to the door, I fell back against the wall. There stood Mary—looking exactly as she had the first day she walked into my studio! Hair cut short, weight back, wearing elderly, unstylish clothes. I wanted to cry or hide as I could not understand why, after I proved to this woman just how beautiful and attractive she could be, she would choose her old ways.

That was the day I grew up and began to understand. I had changed Mary's outside but not the inside. I had not elevated her self-image or personal confidence level at all. I had simply painted over a troubled foundation. I had actually taken Mary out of her comfort zone. She was getting attention with her new look, attention she felt she didn't deserve. She would look in a mirror and say this is not me, I am not attractive, I am not beautiful, and I am not young. Her self-esteem and confidence levels were so low she had to return to who she believed she was.

The Truth About Self-Worth

Self-worth is seeing yourself as a valuable, worthy, capable person who stands for something good. When you look deep inside yourself, you know that most of the decisions you make and actions you take are good. It's a feeling you are of value to the world, and you are in control of your own destiny. People can trust you and openly share what is in their heart. A person with positive self-worth is self-assured and reflects a sense of power, enthusiasm, motion, and accomplishment.

God wants the best for us, but we must first believe we deserve the best. Because we are his very own, he wants us to shine, to be beacons to others, to attract people, to be attractive. God wants us to produce fruit by the way we live. Why is it so hard for us to believe in ourselves, when we believe in a wondrous heavenly Father? *I know I'm not better than anyone, but due to God's forgiving grace and love in my life I know I am as good as everyone.* My self-confidence comes from knowing and accepting that fact.

The day I stood in front of the White House Oval Office and shook hands with the president of the United States, I knew with complete confidence I was not less than but, in the eyes of God, equal to this man. Only the Lord is the final judge and jury on our personage. To anti-age, or age with grace, you must know with confidence you are not inferior to anyone. Understand that the most important opinion of who you are is God's opinion. Your own approval is *also* more important than approval from others.

It is not what you have or own that makes you special, it is what you have become: a loving, generous, kind woman; a woman of tender mercy, kindhearted, considerate, and helpful. A woman who understands the fact that healthy self-confidence and sound self-esteem do not equal *conceited*. To age gracefully, remain true to yourself. Be clear on what you believe and believe in, what you will or will not stand for. To keep those age lines at bay, always live with a clear conscience and make sure your life is in balance. I have seen instant change on the face of women as they discussed the traits that made them special and wonderful. In instances of love lost, "What's wrong with me?" becomes "What on earth was wrong with him? I am a terrific person." It is freeing to your psyche. To slow the aging process the mind, body, and soul must be in harmony with each other. God gave you the ultimate gift, the gift of life, but in order for you to live the ultimate life you must heed the verse, "Love thy eighbor as thyself" (Matthew 22:39 KJV). God is trying to tell you to give your neighbor the same respect and love you feel for yourself. In other words, you must love yourself first, before you can love others in the way he intended.

Others cannot take away our self-respect if we do not give it to them. By choosing actions based on an ethical center, you do not allow another person to compromise your dignity and self-respect. You have the power to choose.

—MAHATMA GANDHI (1869–1948)

Take time to answer each of the following questions honestly. Upon completion you will have a better idea of your level of self-esteem:

1. Do you stand up for your own values and convictions?
2. Do you approach problems and new endeavors free from fear of failure?
3. Do you defer to others on account of their wealth, power, or prestige?
4. Do you allow personal comparisons to affect your sense of self-worth?
5. Do you allow others to talk you into things against your better judgment?
6. Do you meet new people easily?
7. Do you follow every undertaking through to a logical conclusion?
8. Do you walk erect and face everyone with a friendly, open smile?
9. Do you truly believe you are one of God's greatest miracles?

10. Do you truly believe you deserve the finest that life has to offer?
11. Do you sincerely know that your being here on Earth is making a difference?
12. Do you believe you are an inexhaustible reservoir of possibilities?
13. Do you believe you have a song to sing and a story to tell?
14. Do you believe you are very special and that there is no one on Earth exactly like you?
15. Do you believe you were put here on Earth for some special reason?
16. Do you believe that your opinion counts?
17. Do you respect you?
18. Do you feel free from all shame, blame, and guilt?
19. Do you allow the opinions and attitudes of others to hurt you?
20. Do you feel put down when corrected?
21. Do you feel inferior to others?
22. Do you have a strong need for approval and attention from others?
23. Do you need people to agree with you or tell you that you are right?
24. Do you know for a fact it is not what you have or own that makes you special, but what you have become?
25. Do you accept that the major key to a bright future is you?
26. Do you allow yourself the freedom to make mistakes or to be wrong?
27. Do you give yourself the right to say no even when you know it will displease someone?

You must know for a fact you are loved and loveable and that God loves you despite your failures and missteps. He simply loves you because you are you. He loves you as you are—but he loves you too much to leave you where you are. If you base your value on your physical beauty, what happens if you lose it? Even if you feel yourself inadequate or unattractive, God has a completely different view of who you are. God is Judge of your worth on Earth. If you sincerely believe God loves you more than you believe your negative self-talk or feelings of imperfection and weakness, your self-worth will thrive sheltered in his perfect love.

Deep inside every human soul lives the need for respect, and to start to fulfill this need, respect yourself. You can only earn respect by living a life that deserves it. Respect is complicated, as we can truly like another person and enjoy their company but still have little respect for them. Respect is not for sale at any price. You cannot buy respect with money. Respect is earned through actions. Respect is earned over time. People observing your decision-making processes will or will not choose to respect you based on those actions and decisions.

The first questions you must ask yourself are these *Am I worthy of respect, and how many people can I name whom I completely respect?* Webster's definition of *respect* is "worthy of esteem." To gain more self-esteem, you must be a person worthy of respect. It is almost a chicken-and-egg thing. What came first? Self-esteem by definition is *personal value*—how much you value you—your thoughts, your ideas, and who you are as a person. Does your self-worth automatically constitute self-respect? Or did your self-respect produce your self-worth? Any person can derive ego fulfillment from personal accomplishment or station in life—but still be completely void of self-respect.

Self-respect is earned through positive acceptable behavior and actions. The result is confidence, and confidence has a lot to do with aging successfully and slowly. Feeling good about yourself is not conceited—it is *healthy*. God teaches us to be careful not to become prideful, as pride comes before the fall. But pride and self-confidence are two very different issues. I am personally proud of my accomplishments and achievements, but being a child of God, I also know who is behind those achievements, cheering me on. My heavenly Father had a plan for my life and I simply decided to accept his plan.

Knowing who is directing our life's movie should keep us from becoming arrogant or egotistical. *EGO* equals *Easing God Out*. When you leave God out of the equation, you are bound to believe you actually mastered life by yourself.

Personal respect is earned through commendable actions of honesty, morality, trust, and integrity. It is exercising good judgment even when no one is looking or will ever know.

Self-respect adds to the harmony of the human spirit. Self-respect is the one anti-aging force so powerful that very few things created by men of science will ever compare to the simple tranquility such respect gives the heart. Respect for one's own self and for others bring you confidence and contentment. Peace decompresses the muscles of the face. Compare a peaceful face with one filled with anxiety and distress. Peace relaxes the muscles of the face. To find complete peace, one must first find God. Your body belongs to you to do with it what you choose. Your mind, intellect, and knowledge belong to the world, but your soul belongs to God.

Never forget, however, confidence does not mean arrogance. Truly confident people are humble, and humility does not mean humiliation. Humility plus confidence equals inner beauty.

After speaking to and teaching women's groups most of my life, it has become clear to me that self-respect and self-confidence go hand in hand. The more self-confidence you project, the more appealing you are to other people. Self-assured women do not approach aging painfully. They love the freedom it gives them to truly be who they are. You cannot deny the fact that you are enjoying the wisdom and freedom allowed by age. Sadly some women actually suffer mental pain and anguish due to aging.

Accept your position in life, embrace it, and enjoy it. Vivacious people always appear younger, as the muscles of their face have been trained to go up. How it must sadden the Lord to have children who find never-ending fault with themselves! I have an extremely overweight friend who is loaded with self-confidence and has as many friends as she has pounds. The love of the Lord shines through her eyes so brightly you forget her size. Her self-worth is intact, and she is one very happy lady. Self-esteem and self-respect can be owned and enjoyed by anyone, because we are free.

This is Lynn's story. Lynn was my assistant when I held the position of Image Coordinator at Disneyland. As sweet as she was, Lynn possessed little self-worth and thus had a low self-image. Lynn also was the secretary to one of the vice presidents in the company. Due to her personal feeling of inferiority, Lynn never stood out as special, and the vice president was well-aware he could easily intimidate her, which he did on a regular basis.

My office was directly across the hall from the vice president's and next door to Lynn's open office space. Numerous times I would hear the vice president lashing out at Lynn for some minor offense. One day Lynn came to me with tears and said, "Bobbie, what's wrong with me? I try so hard, and he still berates me!"

At that moment, I decided to make Lynn one of my projects. I started with her self-image. First, I began a "compliment campaign." Every opportunity I had I would tell her how great she looked or how a color flattered her skin tone. When she looked as though she had lost a few pounds, I would tell her and comment on how I liked her clothes or outfit.

Lynn began to change. She held her head higher, smiled more, and began to look more fashionable. Her self-image had definitely become more positive. However, the boss remained the same, ever critical. One day I heard an especially loud outburst from the overly stressed vice president. Lynn, once again with tears, came into my office and said, "What's wrong with me? Why can't I please him?"

It was now time to hit the self-worth button. I said, "Lynn maybe there is *nothing* wrong with you. Did you ever consider that maybe something is wrong with *him?*" She looked at me in amazement; she had never considered the possibility he might be the problem. I told her maybe he'd had a fight with his wife, or his children were in trouble. Perhaps it had nothing to do with Lynn. I told her to take a walk to Cinderella's Castle and think about it. Just maybe he was taking out on her his frustrations at a stressful life situation because she allowed it.

Once again I saw the light bulb go on, and she had a big smile on her face; her first big recognition of personal value. She did take that walk, gained personal strength, and instantly lost some frustration wrinkles. About two weeks later, there was another blowup. This time, however, there were no tears when she faced me. I looked up and said, "Okay, what are you going to do about it?" She took a deep breath, turned around, and said to the vice president, "I don't like the way you just talked to me and would appreciate if you never talked to me in that tone again." She spun around, marched out of his office, and shut his door behind her. For the first time in years, she felt powerful and truly confident; her self-worth was growing with every step back to her desk, her self-respect growing to new levels. Lynn did not get fired for taking a stand. Actually she got a raise, and from that moment on, Lynn and Mr. Vice President developed a satisfying, positive relationship.

If you are going to allow other people to walk all over you and treat you with disrespect, whose fault is it? Believe me. You will not feel or look young at 50, 60, or 70 if this is your method of coping with life.

Self-respect is respect for one of God's creations, God's child. That means *you*. Do you know you are a valuable person with something to offer? Do you know you are special? Or do you keep score? I'm better than person A because I have more education, but inferior to person B because she is beautiful. If you have good, sound self-esteem you will not compare yourself with anyone. You are a worthy, contributing person just as you are. You should not need people's approval of you, if you have your own approval. Lynn, my former assistant, lost years off her face once she developed the self-respect she deserved. It was a new beginning and a beautiful thing to watch.

Next we have Jan's story. Jan, an outgoing woman, was kind and loving to others, but it took years of her life to learn how to love and treat herself in the same manner. After 30 years in a miserable marriage, forever sacrificing and denying herself, she could not take it any longer. Her self-esteem and personal value were as low as those of anyone I had ever known. She needed a major shot of confidence and a good lesson in self-love. I invited her for a weekend in my home and prayed I could find the right words to help her understand God's plan for us to live an abundant life. It came to me God had clearly defined for us how we are to love ourselves as well as others.

Love is very patient and kind, never jealous, never boastful or proud, never naughty or selfish or rude. Love does not demand its own way. It is not irritable or touchy. It does not hold grudges and will hardly even notice when others do it wrong. It is never glad about injustice, but rejoices whenever truth wins out. If you love someone you will always be loyal to him no matter what the cost. You will always believe in him, always expect the best from him, and always stand your ground in defending him.

Most of you recognize this passage as the Love Chapter (1 Corinthians 13). I asked Jan to read the words over and over until she understood. This is exactly how God intends for us to love others—but also ourselves; this is important anti-aging advice. Women who have attended my seminars have broken down, tears streaming down their faces, when they realized I was giving them permission to internalize and to accept the Love Chapter, starting by applying it to themselves. Kim, a lovely lady with tears flowing, said, "This class is the first gift I have ever given myself." She had been sacrificing herself 100 percent for her children and boyfriend.

Do you show yourself the kindness you deserve? Are you patient with yourself, or do you believe you must be the perfect wife, mother, or friend? Do you speak rudely to yourself? When you make a mistake do you beat yourself up and say things such as, "Stupid! Why am I so stupid?!"? If you would not say it to a friend, then you should not say it to yourself. And when you do make a mistake do you hang on to a personal grudge? The Bible clearly states we are not to hold grudges and that applies not only to grudges against others, but against ourselves, too. So you made a mistake. Well, who doesn't? Are you irritable? Do you stay mad at yourself most of the time? Do you allow injustices to agitate you?

The Bible says that when you love someone, you will be loyal to that person. Are you loyal to yourself, or do you allow others to walk all over you giving no credence to your thoughts, your ideas, your dreams, and your desires? A woman with confidence and self-worth will speak up when the need arises and defend herself when it is called for. Believe in yourself and the gifts God has bestowed on you. Always expect your best, no matter the circumstances. With your added confidence, you can love yourself as God loves you, unrestrained, with no guilt or self-centeredness. In order to give something away you must first own it. For years I have counseled women and given speeches on the topic, "It's Okay to Think You're Wonderful," because you can't give away something you don't own; I say that with a smile!

Once Jan accepted that the Love Chapter applied to her personally as well as to relationships with others, she began to apply it to her life. Her self-negativity began to fade and as the years have passed, she has become stronger and more confident with each year. Her change to personal approval has changed her face, and she is aging more gracefully. Going through life filled with fear, anger, and resentment will mess up any face. Heed God's words and love yourself as he loves you. God wants you to value who you are. In loving and caring for your body, you are showing reverence for God's creation. By watching your weight and eating right, you are once again showing respect for God's creation. Learn to love your body, the one and only piece of machinery on Earth that can repair itself.

Authentic Love

Here is Christine's story. My dear friend Christine reeks of love and joy. She is a highly intelligent lawyer and law professor who came to my enrichment classes looking for something but wasn't quite sure what. Now a married professional, she lived in a permanent state of agitation and irritation but did not understand why.

As we sat and talked, her story tumbled out. She revealed the joy she had known as a little girl watching her father preach and how that joy had been ripped from her life. Her father decided to continue his education; so he traveled to Berkeley, California, to attend the University of California for his master's in theology. By the end of his studies, he had been stripped of all his former beliefs in the divinity of Christ. He gave up on the Living God, divorced his family, and turned to the practice of Eastern religion.

The effects of his actions were visible on Christine's face. As we continued our conversation, it became clear her father's actions had not only destroyed a family. When he left, he took this little girl's faith in God with him. I asked Christine if she wanted God back in her life. She responded emphatically, "Oh, yes, I feel so empty." We prayed together and a spiritual explosion went off in Christine's heart and soul. She now moves through life differently, and joy surrounds her. Her face has a new look that accompanies her new heart and her new life. Her enthusiasm for her new life of joy has taken years off, not only her face, but also the way she moves. Body language tells us volumes about one's age. She moves younger because she's happy and filled with joy from marinating in God's love.

> *Most important of all, continue to show deep love for each other,*
> *for love makes up for many of your faults.*
> —I PETER 4:8

Some say love is a powerful thing, but love is not a thing. You do not lose it when you give it away. In fact the more you give it away, the more it comes back to you. The best use of life is love. Love is a force so compelling and so mighty it has changed the direction of more lives than history will ever record. The discovery of God's never-failing, precious love and human love completes the circle of love for life. The power of combining spiritual love and human love knows no bounds.

The first inkling I had that Ernie was a man I could love my entire life came to me on a date to a college basketball game. We sat a row in front of five college-age boys, and with each missed basket or disagreement with a referee's call, a long list of expletives came out of their mouths. Finally Ernie had had it. He stood up, turned around, and told these young men to shut their mouths and stop using the language they were using. He said, "I happen to be sitting here with a lady, so shut up!" I knew if any man would face five teenagers to demand respect for my presence, I had a winner. At that time, I was only 17 but old enough and smart enough to realize this man was something and someone special. We have now been married 53 years.

Love is a truly wondrous and magical elixir that floods your body, mind, and soul with the most powerful combination of anti-aging hormones and chemicals known to man. Nothing keeps a woman's anti-aging defenses up like marinating in a totally loving relationship, a loving partnership that gives a feeling of completeness. Since I have been married to the same man since college, this qualifies me as a relationship expert. Personally, I am fed up with authors divorced four or five times writing books on relationship strategies. If those authors had the answers, they would have had one spouse, not several.

Little softens a woman's heart more than having a man tell her in all sincerity just how much he adores and loves her, what a wonderful woman she is, and then confirm those words with actions that prove he means every word he says. The most enticing faces on this earth are the faces of women who have experienced true, authentic love. A woman who has been transformed by having all her emotional needs met is a woman at peace. She is a woman of maturity who has taken responsibility for herself, her decisions, and the condition of her relationships and emotional life. She does not allow abuse or mistreatment of any kind. She understands her personal value as a woman, wife, mother, and friend, but, equally important, so does her man.

Their relationship revolves around mutual respect for one another's differences, allowing each partner to be who they really are. I have often said that if I were eulogizing my husband, I would say, "He allowed me to be me, and I have been one happy woman." Not only did my husband allow me to be me without complaint, he saw my talent and encouraged me to follow my dream. This loving attitude will banish lines from any face. There will be no lines of bitterness or resentment. Do I have lines? Yes— smile lines. Most men want a beautiful woman. With beautiful treatment, he will most likely have just that.

Outside the common-sense information in this book on the external methods I use to slow aging, I am the product of the undeniable love my husband has shown me during the entire length of our marriage. He is tender, caring, and completely devoted to nurturing my mind, heart, body, and soul. I, in turn, have great admiration, respect, love, and affection for him.

The circle of life is complete as we are fortunate to cherish one another just as we are, with all our imperfections. I cannot spell, and he cannot pronounce words correctly. We are perfect for one another; he corrects my spelling and I correct his strange pronunciation of words. We are like many couples who complement each other in the most interesting ways. But it is love that completes our life together. Being born into love, living life in God's love, and dying surrounded by love is the best that life on earth has to offer.

To show my love and gratitude to my husband for his loving kindness, I have worked hard at keeping my figure and weight attractive for him. I take seriously a man's desire for an attractive wife. When I meet my husband's friends I want them to say, "Ernie is a lucky man." Why? Not out of conceit or self-admiration. No, I want to be my best because I respect the man I married and the children we raised. Food is also important to my husband so I lovingly do my best to keep his stomach happy, and I enjoy entertaining his friends.

Nothing releases more anti-aging chemical power than God's love, human love, happiness, and complete peace. Making another person happy also returns to you a rush of healthy emotional feelings. Watching your child jump for joy, helping a family in need, or giving time to charity all produce positive ions.

Medical experts have known for decades that being in a strong, committed relationship enhances one's health and longevity. Our face reflects our story; so we must pay close attention to the emotional and physical needs of the people we love and who love us.

As stated, authentic love is one of the most effective anti-aging medications in our universe. For years, Christopher and Dana Reeve lived on hope and love. There was deep love for one another and hope for the future. Love and hope gave Dana the courage and mental strength to carry on after Chris' death. Discovering her own cancer, she was still filled with love right up to her untimely death. Dana's last contribution to this world was her involvement in a documentary, *The New Medicine*. In her introduction, she tells viewers, "Your emotional state has a tremendous amount to do with sickness, health, and well-being." I have no doubt Dana's love and hope for her husband kept him alive for years beyond the medical professionals' expectations. Love and hope are two four-letter words that carry with them more power than does any anti-aging product ever developed.

Love is the most precious gift any human could give to another. Love fills the empty hole in our heart. Love makes us whole. Love is the most important noun in the dictionary. Turn love into a verb, as love must be acted upon. Love is the one thing you will get more of when you give it away, and it is in the heart of women that much of the love in this world is kept alive.

As we drove down the main street in our town at 9:30 a.m. Christmas morning, not one store was open—not the supermarket, not one service station, not even a store that claimed to be open 24/7. What force could produce the power to overcome greed? The power of love—love brought to mankind through the birth of a little baby born more than 2,000 years ago. One day each year the world seems to slow down just long enough to celebrate love, one for another. My Buddhist friends celebrate Christmas, my agnostic friends stop to celebrate Christmas, and the Muslim donut shop man says, "Merry Christmas!" The only birth in recorded history the world stops to celebrate is the birth of Jesus. Why? Because Jesus was love incarnate.

When the half a billion words we speak throughout our lifetime convey the message, "I believe in you—I appreciate you—I am proud of you—I love you," we are delivering a huge anti-aging stimulant to someone's biological system. Yet no mortal on this earth is capable of comprehending God's capacity to love us.

A psychologist sat beside a little boy playing with Play-Doh. The boy would make a figure into a mom or dad, then take his fist and smash the figures. The psychologist asked, "Why do you do that?" His answer: "People who say they love you are not supposed to hurt you." Oh, the wisdom of a child! The opposite of what hurts us is the powerful language of love. Choose words carefully—heart power is stronger than head power.

The beauty of love is the only thing that lasts forever. When we die, people won't care how much money we made or the degrees we earned. The only thing they will remember is how we made them feel. To anti-age emotionally and spiritually, give love and receive love freely with no strings attached.

After the devastating events of 9/11, a movie documenting the story of United Flight 93 was released. It was obvious the passengers knew they were most likely going to die. In those last minutes, the only thing that mattered to them was confirming their love for their families and the destination of their souls. God tries to reach us all our lives, and I have no doubt many hearts on that plane finally turned to God.

Barbara Walters stated in the December 2005 issue of *Guideposts* magazine, "No matter what religion, people want to know that there is more to life than what is here on earth, that they will be reunited with their loved ones, and that any suffering they've had here on earth is over. It is a place of peace and understanding that will last for all eternity, in union with God. That is what heaven is for. That is the promise of faith." It appears Barbara Walters has searched for and discovered peace and love everlasting for her soul.

The human heart needs to love and be loved. Love is like a mirror—it returns to you what you give it. It is a reflection of your physical and spiritual self, because love comes from your heart. To define love and what it does to us and for us is a monumental task. How does one measure the effects of love on the aging of the body, mind, and soul? What we do know is that without love the world would be a tomb and humanity would self-destruct. The heart is the container of our deepest emotions and highest values.

I was speaking in Texas at a large conference. After I completed my presentation, I went into a lovely lounge to rest a few minutes before heading back to the airport. A young woman in her early twenties walked by, and I commented on her cute, extremely short hairstyle. I told her that her hair looked adorable. She stopped and just stared at me for a moment, then said, "Are you kidding?" I said, "Of course not; you look great."

Having been in my audience, she felt comfortable enough to ask if we could spend a few minutes talking. I agreed, and she told me the most amazing story. Her hair was just growing out after having been shaved for brain surgery to remove a tumor.

She said her father had lived only to get the kids out of the house. There was a complete lack of any kind of expressive love in his life. She said the day of her high school graduation, which he did not attend, she came home to find her suitcases packed and sitting on the front porch with a note that read, "You are now responsible for yourself." She had no place to go but picked up her bags and left. She said she decided one way or another she would find a way to get this uncaring man's attention. One of the first things she did was to get herself arrested for shoplifting. When that didn't work, she continued getting into self-destructive behaviors desperately trying to get his attention. She said, "I became so despondent one day, I just stopped eating. I ended up in the hospital and was near death. I had all kinds of tubes coming in and out of my body when my father finally came to see me."

They visited for a few minutes, then he got up to leave. When he reached the door of her room, she said she lost it and began to scream, "You have never said it. I'm about to die and you still will not say it. I guess you never will." With sarcasm in his voice, he said, "Say what?" She screamed, " 'I love you.' You never have and I guess you never will." I asked her if he ever did say it. She said, "Oh, yes, if he hadn't, I would not be here today. He returned to my bedside, put his head on my bed, and cried like a baby when he realized I was willing to end my life in an attempt to hear those magic words, 'I love you.'"

She told me at that moment their relationship began to heal. For a number of years, she called me to talk about her progress. The last time we talked, the relationship was not perfect, but was now okay, and she would make it.

It is just amazing the power in those three little words. Love is the most preeminent positive emotion we can experience. Love can keep us alive just as hate can destroy us. Love is a powerful medicine.

The Lord has taught us to love and value others as much as we love and value ourselves. It is most obvious that my little Texas friend had a father who had never valued himself and was unable to give away something he had never owned. The human heart is where love lives. In ancient times, the heart was viewed as the seat of humanity. Her father's heart was hard, and only with a softened heart can we learn to love.

If you take only one piece of advice from *Anti-Aging God's Way*, please accept this one: When you love someone, say the words "I love you" daily. To not do so, you are depriving yourself of one of life's greatest joys. God's true test for us—can we love the un-lovable? We all believe in love, but must always remember that *love* is an action word.

Try as you will, you cannot annihilate that eternal relic of the human heart—love.

—Victor Hugo (1802–1885)

Love

Love changes lives
Love beckons
Love invites
Love expands
Love never fails
Love is tender
Love is kind
Love cherishes
Love is alluring
Love is loyal
Love is captivating
Love is powerful
Love is irresistible
Love accepts
Love is non-judgmental
Love is patient
Love adds to everything

Love delivers
Love is merciful
Love nourishes the soul
Love is baffling
Love heals
Love is priceless
Love praises
Love honors
Love is not touchy
Love feeds the spirit
Love does not criticize
Love is a present
Love is everything
Love is ecstasy
Love is a choice
Love awakens desire
Love is action
Love confounds
Love is trustworthy
Love opens a hardened heart
Love says rest in me, be yourself
Love is life
Love heals
Love is never wasted

Look at the heart of a person who knows how to give love and receive love. If you desire a face so youthful that people are stunned at learning your age, above all else make a commitment to nurture the physical, mental, spiritual, and emotional well-being of everyone who comes into your life. Being loved by God and included in his family is the highest honor and greatest reward you will ever receive. Love is the most significant ingredient in a successful life. Even in times of hurt, disappointment, and discontent, love can shine through.

❋ Whom do you love?

❋ What does love do?

❋ What does love say?

❋ How does love act?

❋ When does love start?

Love is experienced through the five senses: seeing, hearing, smelling, tasting, feeling.

Look your best for those you love.

Say words of praise to those you love.

Fill your home with the smell of favorite foods of those you love.

Invite and eat meals with those you love.

Each day hug and hug and hug those you love.

We can live without a hand or foot, a gall bladder, an appendix, a lung, but we cannot live without a heart. Our heart is where love lives, and *love* is the most important word in the dictionary.

Love never fails to deliver results. I am sure we have all heard the stories of the orphanages in Romania. Babies are kept clean and fed, but there is no time to simply hold them and love them. After a short time, the babies learn that crying brings no results so they simply stop crying. First their spirit dies, and then their little souls die, as does their will to live.

Love is a very human phenomenon. Some might say love is passionate affection. Others might believe love is adoration or an intimate relationship between two people. Love is trusting. Love is an act of faith that when we give love, love will be returned to us. To die young at an old age, we must have love in our heart and deep in our souls. If we love in order to get something, then love becomes conditional. As Christians, we must learn to love unconditionally—as God loves us. God gave us perfect love. He gave his all and expects nothing but love in return.

Few humans have the ability to love without expectations. When I married my husband, I was, by today's standards, quite young. I had no expectations except that he would totally and completely love and care for me. Our first home together was an apartment over three garages and across the alley from the town pool hall. We had nothing but complete love to offer one another, but it was enough. With God's blessings, we ended up by the beach in a home I dearly love.

Fifty-three years after that apartment across the alley from the pool hall I am still madly in love with my man. He is a man I can respect. He gives himself completely to me in affection and admiration. I have tasted love at its fullest. I know what real love is, and there is nothing on Earth that will make the face of a woman more beautiful than real, authentic love. When you accept God's love for you and human love for you, that's a winning formula for happiness and real beauty and age control.

A Thought-Provoking Letter

Dear Ann Landers:

Last night I kissed my son and told him that I loved him for the very first time, but he did not hear me because he had committed suicide. I raised my son the way my father raised me and thought it was unmanly for a man to show his emotions. I can't believe how stupid I was. Ann please tell your readers not to withhold their feelings of love from their kids. I will never recover.

Signed:

No name

No city, no state

Part Four

ANTI-AGING BEAUTY SECRETS

Air and Water—
Your Anti-Aging Quick Start

There are two elements the body must have to sustain life—water and air. If you have only water and air, you can still live many days without food. The body must be hydrated and oxygenated to sustain life. How deliberate are you in your actions to do both, to practice common sense toward the two basics elements of life? The human body is 65 percent water. Are you drinking 60 to 80 ounces of water a day? Water hydrates your skin and helps remove toxins from your kidneys, liver, and blood.

Also you need to exercise at least 30 minutes a day to oxygenate your body. "Every day we have over 200 billion red blood cells that are aging and dying" (Body World). Without oxygen, toxins and other wastes build up in our bodies; we become internally toxic and dirty.

To keep the body from prematurely aging, we need to keep our internal organs clean, with clean water and clean air, as most diseases cannot live in an oxygenated environment. When our body gets an optimal amount of oxygen, it also becomes a fat-burning machine. Even if we are not in a position to exercise extensively, we need to take ten minutes to sit quietly and simply breathe. Concentrate on raising your stomach with each breath. Take a breath through your nose, hold it five seconds, and release it through your nose. Deliberate deep breathing is the most inexpensive health supplement we can take because blood transports oxygen to our cells.

Water on the inside is vital to our survival. A plant wilts without proper amounts of water. Take a tip from nature. If you feel wilted, you need to clean out your system with water. Water is the only liquid that allows the liver to rest and cleanse itself. If you want gorgeous skin and clean internal organs, drink water. The good Lord in all his wisdom supplied us with clean air and clean water. Then he made red wine and dark chocolate antioxidants. What a loving heavenly Father we have! Add an ounce of dark chocolate, a glass of wine, and a good night's sleep. Johns Hopkins University has proven that dark chocolate helps prevent heart disease, and for many years, the benefits of red wine have been documented.

From Rock 'n' Roll to Nip and Tuck!

Many years ago, my parents took the family on a summer vacation to visit the capital cities of the western states. As we headed back home to California, our drive took us through Las Vegas, Nevada. At the age of 13, I was completely smitten with the lights and seeming glamour of the place.

Fifty years ago people dressed in beautiful dinner clothes and gowns to gamble in the casinos. Las Vegas had a very different atmosphere from today's casual playground. I concluded I wanted more than a drive through the town. I wanted to get inside one of those casinos.

My parents informed me that no one under 21 years of age was allowed on the gambling floor. Undaunted, I put on what I thought was my best choice of clothes to look older. I grabbed my father's arm and developed my most confident air and positive attitude. Guards would take a second look, then a third, confused I am sure. At six feet tall, they must have assumed I had to be at least 21 years old. What girl was six feet tall at 13? That was a rarity in my youth. Only the tallest show girls were six feet.

At age 13, I was thrilled to think I could pass for 21. Little did I realize then that that feeling would all too quickly evolve into hoping I did not look the age my birth certificate claimed I was. A new pair of jeans and a tight t-shirt, the current fashion of the day—will they make me look younger or stupid? What about a new hair color or eye shadow? Most of us are a little, if not a lot, obsessed with looking the age we feel, not the age on our driver's license. Even men are now obsessed with their appearance, once thought to be only a feminine concern. I am amazed at the number of men who now color their hair and get cosmetic surgery.

On the reverse end from my childhood Las Vegas adventure, I recently requested a senior ticket at my favorite movie theater. The young man looked up and said, "I don't believe you."

I said, "Well, it's true. Do you want to see my driver's license to prove my age?"

He said, "No, but I still don't believe you."That young man did more for my ego than an entire bottle of vitamins A, C, and E. Once again 13 was a lucky number, as I was years into the senior discount category. When we are younger, we are impressed with ourselves if we look older. When we are older, what a thrill it is to be mistaken for younger.

Today we have progressed to the point our breasts can be augmented, reduced, lifted, or even replaced. We can get our fat sucked and injected into another part of our body. We can get nipped, tucked, sucked, lifted, plumped, have Botox and laser treatments, all in an effort to look a little younger and fight the ravages of time. In this fight against old Father Time, we can also break the bank. Renewing or re-youthing can cost many thousands of dollars. Never in the history of the world have bodies undergone so much reshaping. And never have so many cosmetic surgeons driven so many image cars.

Business is booming in the field of anti-aging. Put the word *anti-aging* on any product, and it will fly off the shelves. We cut, we perm, we straighten, and we do our daily 30-minute workout. Then we look in the bathroom mirror and pull on our skin to see how we would look after a little nip and tuck, right? Somehow I think all this obsession must be Eve's fault; after all she was the first female. God in all his perfect handi-work made Eve beautiful and irresistible to Adam. However, after the fall and sin's entrance into Eve's life, perhaps she became dissatisfied with her appearance.

Possibly she saw her reflection in a pond and complained to God about her breast size. Being an ever-loving God wanting to please his children, he made sure the next woman had much larger breasts, only to have her complain about how hard it is to find clothes that fit properly and how her straps cut into her shoulders.

No matter what size or shape, few women see themselves as perfect. No matter how beautiful the supermodel or the movie star, women continue to go under the knife trying to achieve their view of perfection. They're trying to undo all the damage they have done to themselves by over-tanning and under-sleeping, overeating and under-exercising, or over-worrying and under-praying. Cosmetic surgeons are good—but they're not miracle workers.

In my international travels, I have visited some of the most beautiful, majestic houses of worship in the world. The earth is adorned with temples, synagogues, abbeys, mosques, cathedrals, and churches, places where we go to praise a wondrous Creator. How sad and disrespectful it would be if these magnificent buildings were to fall into disrepair! The children of God, however, do not allow these wondrous structures to decay, become derelict, deserted, or abandoned, as that would show great disrespect to our Lord and his houses of worship. When visiting these beautiful architectural wonders, visitors lower their voices, move more slowly, quiet their children, and adopt an attitude of reverence. It is wonderful to experience!

But the really interesting aspect is that God doesn't live there! In reality it's just a beautiful building. God's real home is in the hearts of the people who walk through the doors. God takes up residence in the human heart when invited. He lives inside you and me; this is God's true home. *You* are the temple of God. I do hope you are showing the same respect in maintaining God's human home as you do for a building made of wood or stone.

Working to be the best you can be, not only in your spiritual life but with the human body that houses the spirit of the Lord, is not conceited but respectful. The living body is more magnificent than any building or piece of machinery ever built. No matter how advanced the world of technology becomes, science will never be able to create a machine that strives to repair itself when broken or prays when it is under stress. Live a life that respects the human house of God. Keep it beautiful, keep it clean, and treat it with the same respect as if it were Westminster Abbey.

When I drive down a street in any town worldwide and see the most beautifully maintained home on the block, I assume the home is just as beautiful on the inside as on the outside. That is the way Christian women should approach grooming, beautiful on the outside, beautiful on the inside-respectful to God in every way. Those architectural wonders were constructed with the raw materials of clay, sand, stone, and wood, materials God placed on Earth when he fashioned our world. But it took men and women of vision, talent, and craftsmanship to see what could be accomplished with those raw materials.

Each day when I step into my hour-long bath, I am well aware of the basic equipment God gave me that makes me a woman. Watching what gravity is doing to the equipment is not always pleasant, but the raw materials are there, and it is up to me what I choose to do with them. I thank the good Lord I was not born before the age of powder, blush, eyeliner, and lipstick. My raw materials—skin, hair, and nails—also need the work of a craftsman to keep me presentable. Is it worth the time, energy, and effort? Yes! Yes! Yes!

A man was driving through a desolate part of the countryside when he came upon a beautiful farm. The farmer was in the field, so the traveler stopped and said to him, "What a beautiful farm God has given you!" The farmer replied, "Yes, indeed, but you should have seen it when God had it all to himself."

It is true that God has given us this amazing body, but what we do with it is up to us. We can eat to live or live to eat. We can choose processed foods or natural whole foods. We can exercise or occupy the number-one-selling chair in America, Lazy Boy. We honor God when we show him respect for giving us life by becoming the best we can be mentally, physically, and spiritually.

For you created my inmost being;
you knit me together in my mother's womb.

—PSALM 139:13 (KJV)

It is through God entering your heart you are truly changed. You are now the temple of God, not that building down the street. Love your body, nurture it, be attentive to it, and treat it with tender, loving care. There is little that compares to a loving, peaceful, accepting, contented heart to get you started on a successful anti-aging program.

In our first decade of life, we were pretty little girls. In our second decade, we were lovely teenagers. Entering our third decade, we were beautiful young women. By the end of that decade, we were lucky if someone said, "She is one gorgeous female." The fourth decade is a time of tremendous growth of our understanding of our emotional needs. Reaching our fifth decade, we were attractive for our age. Some women in their sixth and seventh decades are referred to as "handsome women." What on Earth is the definition of a *handsome* woman? Whatever it means I never want to be one. I have always considered my husband to be handsome, and I want him to be the only one in our house who fits that description. However, I will be pleased with "She is very pretty for her age."

If you are in a decade where you will never again hear "gorgeous" on the lips of your admirers, never fear, we are in good company. In the United States, every seven seconds another person turns 50. The United States population has surpassed 300 million and will continue to climb. The population age 85 and over is growing. One day one person in five will be over 65; and I might add that if they follow the suggestions in this book, they will be the best-looking, "youngest" group of seniors—excuse me, "mature people"—yet.

As we age, keeping up with all the new trends can be a full-time job. We might be at the top of the hill, but we're hanging on like crazy. We refuse to believe "over-the-hill" is in sight. For inspiration, we can keep in mind that medical professionals consider today's 50 as yesterday's 30. If that is the way they see it, we might as well believe it, act it, and look it!

My mind might believe I'm still in my 40s, but it forgot to tell my body.

All 78 million baby boomers born in 1946 are now turning 60 at a rate of 8,000 a day, many pretending they are 40 years old (*The Maturing of America* by the National Association of Area Agencies on Aging). I asked a professor when one could be considered mature. He said at age 50. I now question that answer. Boomers will use every method available to fight the aging factor. This is great news for the automobile business, as each day boomers, desperate to redeem their youth, drive new red sports cars off the showroom floor.

This attitude has also done wonders for the health club and spa business. The thought of a woman running down a street sweating like a man who just went twenty rounds with a prizefighter was unheard of until boomers came along. Sweating profusely is now a badge of honor. What was once unladylike is now the order of the day.

If we plan to live past the age of 55, we must be prepared: aging often brings on a few extra pounds. Due to the drop in hormones, and metabolism shifting into low gear, regular exercise is a requirement just to keep our body at its current weight. (My metabolism, once that of a race horse, now resembles a turtle's.)

As I mentioned, often when we are young we strive to look older and sophisticated. In an attempt to look older, some teenagers take up smoking! Not to worry, they will succeed. By age 40, they most likely will have the skin of a 50-year-old and the lungs of a 60-year-old; at 50, they will have the wrinkles of a 70-year- old. The hottest products in skin care today are anti-aging products. This market will continue to grow at a rate of about 20 percent a year. According to Nu-Skin, the anti-aging market is growing $1 million a year.

Many of the "wonder" wrinkle creams will eventually be purchased by teens who are smoking now. Why spend $80 on skin cream, then light up a cigarette (now $6-plus per pack)? If this habit controls you, pray that God will take it away. Any problem you face can be handled with God's help, one day at a time. Depend on God for the strength to overcome any addiction you are fighting.

Pour out your longings before him,
for he can help!
—PSALM 62:8

The LORD longs to be gracious to [us];
He rises to show [us] compassion.
—ISAIAH 30:18 (NIV)

Sleeping Beauty

Sleep is essential not only for your physical and mental health, but for your skin's health. Remember your dark circles and dull skin from lack of sleep during the first few months of your baby's life? It was five long months before I had the joy of sleeping five uninterrupted hours with baby number two. I was almost convinced she wanted to kill me. She was in charge. All she demanded was to be attached to her never-ending supply of mother's milk, and she was content as could be.

Napping has become more acceptable in the United States. Nap if you must, but get your adequate sleep and rest. Health experts say a lack of sleep increases our appetite. When we are tired, we make poor food choices. Have water beside your bed, and hydrate yourself if you awaken. Turn your heat down so as not to rob your skin of moisture. Be sure your face is spotlessly clean and moisturized every night before you sleep. As a relaxer, my husband and I fall asleep with a favorite CD on our Bose.

Another way to look at sleep is that when you are sleeping you are not eating, and that is a good thing. Americans are adding approximately eight pounds per second according to www.Dietdetective.com.

One time after my scales stopped working, I did not rush out to buy a new unit. Without daily weigh-ins, I was totally unaware I was adding weight. At six feet with the weight evenly distributed on my frame, I did not see or feel it until I was in the "Good heavens!" range. How did that happen? I weighed in at 15 pounds over my healthiest weight. On most charts I was okay but not at the weight that makes me feel my most confident. Because of the big M-word (menopause), I had crossed the line and now had to fight to lose the weight. I admit I called my local weight loss center and made an appointment. I lost the weight just in time for my high school class reunion. Needless to say, at my perfect weight, I had a great time.

If your scales have tipped in the wrong direction, it may be aging that is adding a few pounds. As we age, our hormone levels drop, and our metabolism slows. According to data from the Centers for Disease Control, more than 70 percent of people age 55 to 74 are overweight. Of people 70 and older, 60 percent are overweight. This is a clear indication of just how difficult weight management becomes after midlife and menopause. Vow to become one of the 30 percent who maintain a youthful figure and healthy weight.

Eliminating one energy food could change your life. Americans eat between 63 and 150 pounds of sugar a year. That's about 11,250 pounds in a lifetime. My neighbor gave up sugar and lost 30 pounds. I struggle to lose four pounds. How fair is that? When I get to Heaven, I'm heading straight to the complaint department.

Eight hours of sleep is a must. Sleep is the time for the body to heal, renew, and restore itself. Have you ever been with a person who never gets enough sleep? It's not a pretty sight. This person is seldom in a good mood and stresses out everyone around. Sleep is an extremely important element in our anti-aging success story. Sleep is something that cannot be stored up for the future. When we miss sleep, the effect on the body is permanent. Sleeping all day Monday will never fix the damage done by partying all weekend. The body must get its required amount of sleep each 24-hour period. The term "beauty sleep" is indeed accurate and a must. Many emotions and situations cause us to lose sleep, and with every hour lost, aging is accelerated. To ward off premature aging, get your sleep.

As a child, I was taught this simple prayer: "Now I lay me down to sleep. I pray the Lord my soul to keep. If I should die before I wake, I pray the Lord my soul to take." After asking God to bless the family, I drifted off secure in the knowledge I was in God's hands. There are many sleep aids on your drugstore shelf, but perhaps the purpose behind that childhood prayer serves us better: leaving our day's cares with the Lord and turning our soul over to him each night.

Your brain cells talk to each other by means of chemical messengers. When you are exposed to too much stress, chemical communications in the brain begin to fail, causing sleep disturbance, aches, depression, and anxiety. Stress levels in our society are increasing, and as a result, sleep problems are also increasing. This is not good. If you continue a pattern of too little sleep, permanent damage may be done.

How you sleep is also a factor. Little lines once began to appear on the right side of my face, especially by my mouth, and I was having painful problems with my neck. The pain became so serious I was unable to turn my head, yet not one of the doctors asked me my favorite sleeping position. I was sleeping on my stomach with my head turned to the left. I was causing my own wrinkles and pain. One day, my daughter asked me how I was sleeping. When I told her, she yelled, "You can't do that!" What I discovered was one of the best anti-aging techniques known—sleep on your back. When I changed my sleeping position, all my neck pain vanished and slowly the lines began to diminish from my face.

Sleep regenerates your energy, fixes broken cells, and heals and refreshes your body. Carrying a load of stressful problems causes additional wear and tear on the body; therefore, adequate sleep is a must.

As a child, being taught to take my problems and cares and give them to God each night before sleep was priceless. No one on Earth has the power to love me or care about my problems, needs, and wants more than does the Lord. Carrying around a heavy load of problems is certain to cause wear and tear on the body. In ancient times, the Indians were taught to dig a hole in the ground, speak into the hole all their problems, then cover up the hole, quickly burying all those problems in Mother Earth and leaving them there. Personally, I cup my hands together, fill my hands with my problems and visualize laying them in the Lord's lap. Do whatever works for you, but don't carry a load that is causing your shoulders to droop and your posture to say, "I'm old."

Life and sleep will come much easier when you faithfully believe the Creator of all things beautiful has your life in his hands. Your body is made up of trillions of cells. Each cell has a short life span, from a few weeks to a few months. A stem cell's job is to maintain and repair tissue. As we expose ourselves to environmental assaults, such as too much sunshine, our stem cells die off and lose their ability to regenerate our skin. Our skin loses its elasticity. Elastin, a protein in our skin, is like a rubber band: once damaged it can no longer bounce back. The same goes for the skin. Damaged elastin means wrinkled skin.

Ultraviolet (UV) radiation comes to us at all times of the year. Regardless of the time of day or season of the year, the sun's rays can damage your skin. Water, snow, sand, and light-colored rocks reflect sunlight and damage the skin the same way sunbathing does after only 15 minutes.

You may believe that, not living in the Sun Belt, you have little exposure to the sun. As an example, let's say you are only exposed to the sun 15 minutes a day. Multiplied by 365 days a year, that equals 5,475 minutes (about 91 hours) a year of sun damage to your skin. If you live to be 70, that equals 383,250 minutes (about 266 *days*) of sun damage to your stem cells.

If you eat junk food, sit most of the day, get little exercise or sleep, and are stressed, you have most likely condensed your life span. One of the most fascinating revelations of the last decade is that emotions change our cells through the same molecular process as exercise. Emotional stress causes serious damage to our cells.

The good news is there is an ever-loving and caring heavenly Father ready to take on our problems. We should not allow everyday stress and emotions to damage those precious life-giving cells—so leave your problems with the Lord. You can have faith that moves mountains, but God must have your full cooperation when it comes to issues of your health. Faith without action is no faith at all.

The longer I live, the more I realize common sense is not very common. Isn't it common sense to heed what God says about rest? He actually set one day aside. The total purpose of doing so was to teach us that the body needs rest, complete rest.

The word *Sabbath* means "rest." We are to remember the Sabbath day to keep it holy. God commands us to keep one full day to be deeply centered on God, your beliefs, and your practice of religious faith. We are to remain reverent and respectful to the Lord's Day.

The Bible tells us to keep Sunday as a sacred day, but we work, keep our malls open, go see R-rated movies, spend hours in front of the TV, or paint the house. We spend hours at the soccer field or on the golf course. Monday, it is back to the usual grind of work and school. That day of complete rest in the Lord never happened. We ignore God's laws. We do not give over one day exclusively to search for purpose in our lives. Why do we age prematurely? We break rules. No wonder we are so stressed!

Remember the Sabbath day by keeping it holy. Six days you shall labor and do all your work, but the seventh day is a Sabbath to the LORD your God. On it you shall not do any work, neither you, nor your son or daughter, nor your manservant or maidservant, nor your animals, nor the alien within your gates. For in six days the LORD made the heavens and earth, the sea, and all that is in them, but he rested on the seventh day.

—EXODUS 20:8 (NIV)

We are stressed as a nation because we break the rules. We are personally stressed because we break the rules. God gave us the Ten Commandments to make our lives easier, but we break the rules and suffer the consequences. Common sense? I don't think so.

The Secrets of Beautiful Skin

Obsession with our appearance is hardly a new phenomenon. But we now live in a totally visual world of television, phone, and computer cameras, so we feel compelled to take our appearance to new heights. Dwight D. Eisenhower was our last bald president.

We once judged people on character through long-term relationships. Sadly, we now use our eyes to make our judgments of people. Most women would love to look younger than their actual chronological age, but sitting on the couch, hoping that this will magically be our destiny, is not realistic. Cheating Father Time has many components; both emotional and physical health affect how well you age. Nutrition and exercise affect how well you age. Sun damage and skin care affect how well you age; overall happiness and attitude affect how well you age; and smoking *definitely* affects how well (or poorly) you age.

Looking younger than your actual age takes desire, attitude, long-term strategies, work, and immediate action. My number 1 rule for achieving a beautiful complexion and dissolving away years from your face is letting God's radiance shine through. Start by letting the joy of his light radiate through your eyes. Illuminate the world with the peace, joy, and love you know in Christ Jesus. However, you must do your part, too. God has supplied us with every essential nutrient your body and skin will ever need, but it is up to you to find what works.

Our passion to maintain a youthful appearance has driven the anti-aging market to more than $1 billion a year. We fantasize we can buy a cream and, like magic, kiss those wrinkles good-bye. Unfortunately, it's just not that simple. And unfortunately, millions of dollars are being wasted on products that just don't work. The price of a product has no relevance to how well it works. More expensive does not necessarily mean more effective.

Today's Sun Worshipper, Tomorrow's Prune

You cannot have the skin of a 30-year-old when you are 50 and at the same time, spend hours sunbathing. There is only so much a body can do to repair itself if you insist on overexposing it to the drying effects of the sun.

Let us look at a perfect plum—a ripe, crimson plum. Leave it in the sun, and it turns magically into a prune—a dark brown, shriveled-up, wrinkled prune. The lowly prune has such a bad image, they are no longer even called prunes. The producers now label them "dried plums." Whatever we call them, it is the same end result: a dark brown, shriveled-up, wrinkled fruit.

After our plum has spent hours in the sun, let's try to repair the damage. Start by rubbing oil all over the prune, and all you have gained is an oily piece of fruit. Next, rub moisturizer over the prune for a solid month. It still cannot be returned to its original plum self. Now take the prune and plunge it into water. After a long time, the prune has done its best to absorb a little of its lost beauty and fullness, but all that remains is an overexposed, soggy, second-rate, shrunken plum. It is a prune—never to become a plum again.

Sun is good for us, but we must limit our exposure to no more than two hours a day, before noon or after 4 p.m. On Waikiki, I saw a woman who had at one time been the hottest babe on the beach, still thin and trim and wearing a small two-piece swim suit. Her skin was the color of dark brown sugar, her hair still long and blonde. Off she went, headed for another day on the beach with her surfboard under her arm. Her skin and that deep, dark tan might have been beautiful at 18 but today, 50 years later, she was indeed the perfect example of a one-time plum, now a prune. Her skin was so wrinkled there was not a smooth inch on her entire body. When skin becomes damaged or leathery, it ages faster. Our cells become less flexible and can no longer receive nutrients as easily. People were still staring as they did 50 years earlier but now for a very different reason. (Part of me, however, admired her spirit.)

There are numerous anti-aging strategies we must consider. Unfortunately, I have not found a pill that will keep my thighs from spreading twice their size when I sit down or a cream that will tighten the skin on my elbows. As we age, the skin on our elbows begins its imitation of a Shar-Pei puppy.

I heard that the Chinese tell a woman's age by the number of wrinkles on her elbows, one wrinkle for every ten years. I guess that means long sleeves for me from now on. All kidding aside, I found the theory to work. Few women have received arm-lifts or fat transfer into their hands, even though they are becoming a new trend. The face can be lifted, but the hands and elbows can present a problem for aging-obsessed people.

Aging slowly is about creating conditions in your body that will allow your cells to receive all the nutrients and oxygen they must have to survive. Never go into the sun without at least a 30 SPF sun block. By age 40, most women start showing signs of skin and sun damage: wrinkles around the eyes or mouth or dark age spots from overexposure to the sun (or, worse yet, from tanning beds). Every UV ray damages the collagen in your skin. What the age-conscious should be spending their money on are sunscreens and/or instant tanning lotions. Once your skin has been damaged from smoking or too much sun or lack of attention, it then takes a great derma-tologist to undo the destruction.

Tests conducted on more than two hundred women by one of America's most prestigious testing laboratories found the *most* expensive anti-aging, anti-wrinkle creams to be the *least* effective. According to studies, one of the highest-rated, most effective, and also the most affordable was Olay Regenerist.

How do you find your perfect combination of products for vibrant, flawless skin? Trial and error? One option is to visit a plastic surgeon, and wipe away 10 years. However, if through the years you have been dedicated to and diligently following a routine to prevent premature aging, you may presently look 10 to 15 years younger than your actual age. If you choose medical treatments on top of what you have already accomplished in the anti-aging department, you may eliminate another 10 years, and wouldn't you love that?

On a recent trip to San Francisco, my husband's business associate, whom I had never met, assumed I was my husband's second and younger wife by 25 years. My husband has become accustomed to this assumption during our many years of marriage. I tell this only to motivate you to start today. Set a goal and make one small change after another until all the factors that prevent premature aging become habits.

I am not opposed to using the wonders of modern medicine, if you feel that is your only option. However, by starting early and using common sense and discipline, your anti-aging skin goals will be accomplished in a more natural way. If you feel your parents cheated you out of the perfect skin gene, don't get mad, get busy. I will walk you through not only my daily routine but my personal beliefs on methods to slow the aging process.

I would like to make it clear I am not a doctor or a nutritionist. I am a professional woman with one husband, two children, and six grandchildren who has accomplished her goals in the anti-aging department. It may take you time, willingness, practice, and patience to balance your life and achieve the principles outlined in the preceding sections of this book, but do not give up. Set your goals and keep your focus.

Let's get started on your skin's anti-aging program. Your skin, like the other organs of your body, regenerates and heals while you sleep. Therefore, I am very diligent about my nighttime skin care routine.

Olive Oil— Inside and Outside

An anti-aging ritual is as easy and quick to start as driving over to your nearest Costco or market and buying two bottles of good organic extra virgin olive oil: one bottle for the kitchen and one bottle for the bathroom. By now you know about God's special blessing to us, the olive tree. The Mount of Olives plays a prominent role throughout the earthly life of Jesus, as well as in his ascension and his return. Taken internally, olive oil protects your heart, promotes weight loss, combats cancer, and battles diabetes. Olive oil also smoothes your skin. The oil of the olive should play a significant role in your life, health, and skin care plan. Use extra virgin olive oil to remove your foundation makeup every night. Now entering my seventh decade, I can honestly say my skin (minus a few lines) has never been in better condition. My commitment to olive oil products began with a free sample sent to me in the mail.

My Nightly "Four-Step" Bedtime Ritual

Step 1. I rub organic extra virgin olive oil all over my dry face to loosen the day's dirt, excess oil, and foundation makeup. (Put your olive oil into a six-ounce pump to make it easier to use.) Pump a squirt into your hand, and rub it from your hair line to the bottom of your neck. I allow it to sit on my face from 30 seconds to a minute. I then take two or three unscented baby wipes to remove as much foundation makeup as I can.

Step 2. I use a mild olive oil soap or Neutrogena Deep Clean Gentle Scrub to remove any traces of foundation left on my face. I promise your face will not feel as if you just fell into your salad bowl. Your face will feel smooth and clean, and you will have happy skin. Follow the cleansing with a splash of your favorite alcohol-free, mild toning lotion. Toning prepares your skin for your anti-aging creams and lotions; it is your passage between cleansing and moisturizing.

Step 3. Use your favorite mascara remover. Personally, I prefer baby oil and pressed cotton rounds for the removal of mascara. Once your mascara is removed, take a drop of Squalane, and pat it around your eyes. Squalane is a pure olive oil product. Always use a moisturizer, even if your skin is oily.

Step 4. Apply your treatment creams and lotions. Every night I apply Olay Regenerist Alpha Hydroxy with collagen, Co Q10, and fade cream on any brown spots. Your skin has multiple layers stacked on top of each other.

The bottom layers are fluffy and alive. The top layers, called *stratum corneum,* are dead layers. Your skin is constantly renewing itself, so those dead layers must be removed.

Most moisturizers penetrate the stratum corneum but do not penetrate the living skin underneath. As the top layers lose moisture, fine lines appear. Alpha Hydroxy acids, derived from milk, fruits, and sugar, can help shed dead skin cells. Professional dermabrasion or chemical peels do wonders to shed dead skin cells. The result is a fresher, younger appearance. I have found it just as effective to consistently apply my Alpha Hydroxy acid. I must stress that your skin care is not a hit-or-miss situation—it needs to be done every night. That is what makes it successful year after year. These procedures will make wrinkles less evident. Your objective is to consistently slough off the dead skin.

By now, I am sure you have heard about coenzyme Q10. Q10 is found in every cell in your body. This antioxidant nutrient is involved in producing energy within your cells. Q10 naturally occurs in youthful skin and begins decreasing around age 30. Because coenzyme Q10's ability to penetrate the skin is exceptional, apply more than one application before bed if your skin is extremely dry. Q10 helps bring back moisture; it regenerates, rejuvenates, and restores suppleness while fighting free radicals. Q10 helps minimize damage due to UV rays while promoting elasticity.

While in a Japanese market on a trip to San Francisco, I saw a bottle of Q10 lotion. I still have no idea what the bottle says, as it is written in Japanese, but I use it *every* night.

I recently met friends for lunch. Their first comment was, "You had some work done to your face. What did you do?" (In Orange County, California, it is not considered rude for friends to ask if you had facial work done; it is almost a badge of honor.) First thinking they were referring to something surgical, I said no. It was only later I began to realize it was the effects of the Co Q10. My skin is definitely more radiant.

The beauty industry sells billions of dollars of products each year. Organic Monitor states global natural cosmetics revenues have surpassed10 ten billion US dollars this year alone (www.npicenter.com). Since the skin is the body's largest organ, it is natural that we are concerned about our skin's youthfulness, health, and appearance. The skin-care industry develops thousands of new products a year. Whatever your skin type, there are products for you. Again, it is a matter of trial and error to find the right ones.

Somewhere out there a marketing company has zeroed in on my birthdate and theorized because I am not dead, I must need a lot of health and skin aids. The latest brochure offered 70 of what they called basic health care needs for as little as $5 to $64. No matter what the problem, they had the answer. They promised that if I would just try one bottle of their magic formula, I would turn the clock back 30 years. I don't think so!

Since I investigate products, I called for a free sample. All the company asked for was a credit card number for the shipping. As I listened carefully to the salesperson's rapid pitch, it became clear that once they had my credit card number, they would automatically charge my credit card $60 each month, and send me my monthly supply of their phenomenal anti-aging cream, whether I ordered it or not. I informed the man in no way would I fall for that scam. Anti-aging and anti-wrinkle are the new superwords, so proceed with caution.

Exercise is also a major part of my skin care program. When you exercise, you take in more oxygen. Your blood cells transport the oxygen throughout your body, which will increase your energy and make you look and feel younger. Therefore, make sure those precious red blood cells work like the Energizer bunny to keep you going. To complete your skin's nourishment, add vitamins A, E, and C. Visit your dermatologist at least once a year, and add a facial to your regimen every few months.

Each morning weigh yourself immediately after you wake up and before you eat breakfast. This is the best time to step on the scales to get your accurate weight. Some experts do not find a need for daily weigh-ins but for anyone over age 40, I believe it is necessary. We all know losing weight is difficult, but keeping the weight off is the *real* challenge. Each day after my weigh-in, I use the information to plan that day's activity (spending more time on the treadmill or cutting back on my treats).

Take into consideration that water retention or salt intake can cause your weight to fluctuate by several pounds. Weighing daily will help keep you on track. According to studies conducted by researchers at Brown University, daily weigh-ins help us lose weight or maintain our ideal weight once we reach it. Purchase a set of scales that measures your weight in half-pound increments. With daily weigh-ins, think in terms of half-pounds. Lose a pound a week. This is not insurmountable, but the thought of tackling 50 pounds is staggering. Assuming you lose one pound a week, at the end of one year, you would be 52 pounds lighter. How hard is it to lose a half-pound? *Only about one dessert or a 45-minute walk.*

Extra pounds truly age us. God fashioned women, his beautiful creations, to have a waist. Vow right now to get your waist back. Dr. Oz tells us our waist measurement should never be more than half our height. Okay, my beauties, hit the treadmill or deliberately drop things on the floor so you must pick them up. Or stand up at each TV commercial and twist from side to side. Make whatever you do fun, make it a goal, challenge yourself, develop a little discipline, and drop unwanted pounds.

Many people will tell you that today there are more overweight people in the world than starving people. Most of America is overweight. The average woman in America is 5'4" and 164 pounds. I do not believe the only way to a healthy weight is a gym membership. All we need is a brisk walk for 30 minutes a day to maintain our present weight. If you want to lose weight, however, you need to take 10,000 steps a day. If that sounds impossible, it is not. I wear my pedometer to count my daily steps. Exercise is your body's best medicine throughout your life.

As we age, it becomes even more important that we get our proper amount of exercise. Exercise boosts your immune system. Even if all you can find time for is a walk around the block, take that walk. Weight-bearing exercises are even better. Lifting weights burns calories and fights the loss of muscle that occurs in aging. You do not have to go to your local gym if it makes you feel uncomfortable. Simply take a pillow case, throw a couple of good- sized books inside and lift, or fill a couple of old pots with sand and lift. When it becomes easy, add more books or sand.

Here is an easy anti-aging exercise for your posture. While walking, find a straight line or shadow. Walking normally, use this line as a guide for foot placement. This simple exercise helps with your balance. As we age, we have the tendency to walk with legs apart and feet pointed outward for balance. Start now to develop a perfectly balanced body. Tai chi or stretching exercises can help. A straight body, head held high and perfectly balanced—that's what we call beautiful posture.

America has certainly changed in the last four decades. In my childhood, people were seldom overweight. I only recall one woman in the congregation of our large church who would have been considered obese. Because we are so stressed, we are eating too much comfort food. Or is it due to those beautiful flat screen HD television sets we sit in front of? Jesus had to walk everywhere he went, so he had the secret of maintaining his weight by default. Jesus had no car in the driveway or taxi on the corner. He walked. So make a vow now to be more like Jesus not only spiritually, but physically as well.

Each day, take time to renew your body, mind, and soul. It is only by balancing these areas that we are superior to animals. Never forget that improving your appearance honors God. You are the only you that you will ever have; so become the best you can be.

My Private Sanctuary

After breakfast, I suggest a wonderful, relaxing bath. Fill the tub as high as you can, using medium warm to hot water. Overly hot water dries your skin. I can hear some of you saying, "What?! I have no time for a bath." If there is one thing longevity and age have taught me, it's that people always find time to do exactly what they deem important.

Ask a friend to serve on a charity committee, and she has no time. Ask the same friend to spend a week with you in Palm Springs or your favorite ski resort and, lo and behold, she finds time! Just about every person does exactly what she wants to do with her time.

I am suggesting that a leisurely morning bath beats a rushed shower any day, so get up an hour earlier. In all my years of professional speaking and traveling around the world, I've never changed that very important part of a good beginning to my day. When our girls were pre-kindergarten, my hour in the bath tub was directly after dinner. I called it "Daddy's time with the girls," and, needless to say, my husband enjoyed a sweet-smelling, freshly bathed wife at bedtime.

Having switched from after dinner to mornings, I now use the time to make and receive business phone calls. I put a mirror on the ledge around my bathtub and apply my makeup in the natural light of the window, all the while soaking in my Vitabath bubbles. At times, I fix my bowl of oatmeal while the tub is filling and eat my oats in the tub. Don't knock it if you have never tried it! Your day starts relaxed, you are nourished, and your face is completely made up. Consider all the multitasking going on here! Relax and use your tub time to view problems as opportunities to achieve. In your tub, ask God to bless your day, your family, and your friends.

While bathing, celebrate your own uniqueness. Think about the fact that you are the only you who will ever grace this earth. No one on Earth has your DNA, fingerprints, personality, or sense of humor. No one on Earth is exactly like you. You are a one-of-a-kind original—you are special and unique.

In your tub, face your life with optimism, enthusiasm, and faith in an all-loving God. While relaxing, enjoy God's sense of humor as you look at your skin getting a little looser by the day. Make this bath time a fabulous experience and a daily part of your anti-aging plan. If your skin appears dry, use a Body Butter by Sensaria. This is a fabulous product. It penetrates the skin immediately and never feels greasy or oily, and it smells wonderful.

Immediately after your bath, attach a pedometer to the waist band of your clothes to count those daily steps. That one little practice will have a very positive outcome on your weight-control program. Strive for those 10,000 steps. You will be surprised by the change in your attitude. Instead of looking for the closest parking spot at the supermarket, you will pick one far away from the entrance to help you achieve your goal. When I don't reach the 10,000 mark, I'll try for 5,000 and head to the gym and get on the treadmill for a stroll. The optimal word here is *stroll*. I suggest you forego running, as running can change the direction your lovely breasts face. However, if you prefer running to strolling, be sure you wear one of the best sports bras made. Years and gravity have a way of redirecting breasts in a southerly direction. Yes, running can speed weight loss, but it can also speed the change in the direction those breasts face. Forward is our goal. My friend Christine believed, as she was small-breasted, she did not need to wear a bra. She now tells me, "darn," gravity is gravity.

Keep Current

Keep yourself current by scanning the day's news, but be discriminating, and avoid filling your head with negative news. My favorite regular column in my *Orange County Register* newspaper is entitled the "Morning Read." It is a positive feature on people who contribute their best to society or who have overcome amazing odds and won. It is uplifting and helps me concentrate on the good life. That is what God wants for us. It took me years to convince my husband I did not want a report on all the murders, or the child, wife, or pet abusers in our community, and I certainly did not wish to take the sins of the world's inhabitants on my shoulders every day.

Pretend, if you must, that more good and love abounds throughout this world than evil. To age gracefully, pick what you read, listen to, or see on the movie screen with thought and care. If people question your positive attitude, tell them you desire to live in the peremptory, assertive belief that humans are good and kind. When my associates or family members make a negative statement or comment, I do my best to turn it around to a positive. What I'm attempting to do is protect myself against negatively polluted energy. There is so much negativity in this world! If you allow negativity to become your focus, it will cause aging at a super-high speed.

You are now relaxed from your bath, you have a great attitude, your face is made up, and your hair is in place. Now dress with style. Add a few distinctive accessories, and watch the heads turn. If by chance you run into a former sweetheart, make him sad he let you go.

Just Like American Express— Don't Leave Home Without It!

Perhaps applying color to enhance one's features began in the jungles of Africa or in the beautiful majestic palaces of Greece. Without makeup, I know I would never have achieved the success I have known. Makeup need not be expensive. It is skill in application that turns heads. I know of women who only apply makeup for a special occasion. The average life span is 28,500 days; so make every one of them special for your family and your business associates. If you have passed age 25, it is time to consider makeup to enhance your best features.

Few women are blessed with such natural beauty that they can go through life a la natural, but the bulk of your beauty budget should be spent on good skin care products and/or treatments, not makeup. Exceptional skin care products are as near as your drugstore. Many of America's top dermatologists use Olay, Cetaphel, Aveeno, Neutrogena, Ponds, Remora, or Johnson & Johnson, just to name a few. It is all about proven ingredients.

To learn new makeup techniques, visit local department stores, such as Nordstrom, Macy's, or Neiman Marcus. Have one of the cosmetics representatives apply your makeup. Go to a different store each week until you find your best look. Ask questions, get advice, and take note of the compliments you receive. Now, armed with your new knowledge, head to your drugstore. Duplicate the products you've learned about, using Revlon, Lancôme, Cover Girl, or whatever brand suits you. My two beautiful daughters and I have never found it necessary to purchase cosmetics anyplace but our neighborhood drugstore.

I will color my roots or style my hair, but there is one part of looking well-groomed I leave to the professionals: my finger nails. Beautifully manicured nails, hands and feet, are a must. And a beautiful piece of jewelry always helps make hands look younger. Hands give away our age quicker than a lightning bolt. Take care of your hands and nails with the same obsession you do your face. Buy a jar of fade cream and use it twice daily. My 94-year-old father eliminated age spots from his hands and arms simply using fade cream. Just as with sunscreen on the face, each day apply sunscreen to the back of your hands.

Unfortunately, many decisions are made on appearance, right or wrong. People tend to equate a tastefully manicured appearance with intelligence and self-respect—appearance and grooming do matter. Actors were once the prime candidates for youth-renewing plastic surgery. Today men and women alike, in every industry, believe the younger and more youthful the appearance, the greater your chances of winning the race up the corporate ladder. Be it a political race or a job promotion, Americans are youth-obsessed, spending billions of dollars a year in various body improvements. Do what you need to do to be the best you can be.

A Quick Review

1. Organic virgin olive oil to remove makeup.
2. Wipe off with unscented baby wipes.
3. Wash with a mild soap.
4. Tone and moisturize skin.

5. Using baby oil, remove all traces of eye makeup. Dot eye area with Squalane.
6. Apply treatment lotions.
7. Before bed, apply fade cream to hands to prevent age spots.
8. Turn down the heat.
9. Make sure the place where you spend one-third of your life is comfortable. Perhaps a pillow top mattress would be beneficial for a great night's sleep.
10. Hydrate (drink water) during the night, and sleep on your back.
11. Each day: wake up rested, weigh in, and thank God he has given you yet another day to try to get this living thing right.
12. Head to the bubble bath or Vitabath, sink up to your chin, count your blessings, and talk to your heavenly Father.
13. The only reason not to use sunscreen under your foundation makeup: you are too sick to even venture past the bedroom door.
14. Dress as if you care about how you look.
15. Have a blessed, relaxed, unstressful day, and watch the years fade away from your face.
16. Do the best you can to put 10,000 steps on that pedometer.
17. Get a spritz of your favorite perfume.
18. Take the weight of the world off your shoulders, or they will droop.
19. Thank God that you live in a free country.
20. Make as many statements during the day as you can where the other person must answer, "Thank you."
21. And remember—the only reason to have children is to enjoy them. So enjoy them.
22. Protect your hands from sun damage by using a sunscreen.

A Few of My Favorite Products

A pearl drop of Neutrogena Healthy Skin Anti-Wrinkle SPF 15 mixed with a pearl drop of Neutrogena Healthy Defense daily moisturizer light tint SPF30 under Revlon Color Stay foundation makeup SPF 6. This not only protects my skin from UV damage all day; but the Retinol in the anti-wrinkle cream continues the sloughing of old skin, bringing up the supple new skin all day as well.

To truly check the condition of your skin, buy a 10x to 15x mirror.

For dry skin on your body, use Sensaria Body Butter. Apply immediately after bath or shower when skin is still damp and pores are open.

Because our eyes tell our story, be sure to spend time each day on enhancement. My favorite mascara is L'Oréal Telescopic Explosion with its round brush.

If you feel you are too old to spend 15 minutes a night and a few minutes each morning with these routines, think again! Aging actually begins the minute you stop growing. It is best to start thinking about wrinkles in your twenties, but few young people give it much thought until they look closely at themselves in a mirror and see their mother. So you are 40, 50, 60, or 70. You can still look 40 when you're 50, 60, and 70, but you must commit yourself to and begin a *daily* skin care ritual now. Look forward to the compliments you will receive. As there were few anti-aging creams during my mother's earlier life, she simply used petroleum jelly daily and looked 70 at 90.

Wonderful new products like L'oréal Studio Secrets and Revlon Photo Ready give your skin a smoother appearance. I like the results they give me.

To top off my list, I am a huge fan of the Regenerist products by Olay. You simply do not have to spend hundreds of dollars on high-end products. Affordable products work just as well. Look for products with retinoid and sunblock.

Preventing Osteoporosis— Through Food and Exercise

As we age, osteoporosis often becomes a problem. In the Chinese language, there is no word for osteoporosis. The cultures who obtain their calcium from vegetable sources have a very low incidence of osteoporosis. So, ladies, eat those veggies! Soy can also help prevent osteoporosis and help alleviate the symptoms of menopause.

One Diet Coke a day sounds harmless, right? That is what I thought until I read a recent study of 2,500 women. With every cola we drink, we lose a little bone mass. The more cola a woman drinks, the weaker her bones become. Daily cola drinkers were most affected. Whether diet, regular, or caffeine-free, the same results occur. The problem ingredient is phosphoric acid, which is not found in all soft drinks. This study was authored by Katherine Tucker, senior scientist and director of the Dietary Assessment and Epidemiology Research Program at Tufts University. Phosphoric acid may temporarily increase the acidity of the blood, which the body neutralizes by leaching calcium from our bones. Giving up cola drinks is a small price to pay for keeping our bones strong.

Exercise, especially weight-bearing exercise, is another method to help prevent osteoporosis. Simple aging weakens your bones. Add smoking, excessive alcohol consumption, and/or some medications, and osteoporosis may be in your future.

A 1993 editorial in the Journal of the American Medical Association suggested women should triple their daily intake of calcium to lower the risk of osteoporosis. A woman needs from 1,000 to 1,500 milligrams of calcium a day, depending on age. You may want to take a calcium supplement, especially if milk products upset your stomach. Still, the best way to get your calcium is to eat salmon, sardines, yogurt, and green vegetables.

Posture

Body language and posture define your self-image and your apparent age long before anyone is close enough to see your face. Slumped shoulders, head tilted forward, rounded back; short, shuffling steps; legs separated with feet turned out are all signs of aging posture.

Face maintenance and/or plastic surgery can be effective for a youthful appearance only if your body's movement and posture re-enforce the age of your face. Standing tall and straight with ears over shoulders, and shoulders over hips, is the proper stance. Here is an easy exercise I use to keep my posture youthful. Stand with your feet six inches apart and twelve inches away from a flat wall surface. Bend your knees slightly, bend over, and let your spine fall against the wall. Keeping your knees bent, slowly roll your body up the wall until it is completely flat. Now slowly straighten your knees, again keeping your back flat, and press hard against that wall. Last, slowly pull your feet back toward the baseboard as close as you can while keeping your back up against the wall. Hold this position as long as is comfortable.

Clean Colon

Your colon is home to toxins that can cause problems, from fatigue to headaches to bad breath. Over time, an unclean colon can slowly destroy your health. To cleanse your colon, get the proper amount of liquid, fiber, and exercise.

Many years ago, I concluded that the reason for my husband's unbelievable health was his colon. His colon was forever clean. His body rids itself of toxins three to four times a day. He appeared to be a detoxification machine. He has never paid much attention to diet. He was simply blessed with a body that efficiently cleanses itself. As unpleasant as you may feel about this information, after living with the results of what a clean colon can do for your health, I became serious about achieving the same results. With a constant water bottle at my finger tips and adequate fiber, I achieved the same results: an active, clean colon that cleanses itself several times a day. And when it comes to a clean colon, God gave us the natural cleanser—prunes.

Balance

I highly suggest you give yourself a gift of massage. A good massage therapist can do wonders to help balance your body, relax your muscles, rid your body of stress and/or pain, plus get your blood circulation moving.

Most of my life, I suffered from severe back pain due to a childhood accident. Through the years, I have worn back braces, been plastered into a body cast, and been given shots and chiropractic adjustments. Then one day I found "Helen," a massage therapist who specializes in bad backs. My once uneven shoulders are now level, and I have experienced real pain relief with her techniques.

Massage therapy dates back thousands of years to when natural healing was the remedy of the times. References to massage have been found in writings from ancient cultures such as Egypt, China, Greece, and Rome. Those serious about anti-aging understand the balance of mind, body, and soul.

Clean Blood

Sunday meant church in my family. My earliest memories revolve around church events and Sunday school. When you are taught Christian doctrine from childhood, you become aware of the significance of blood. I listened, I learned, and became very conscious of the large part that blood plays in our religious beliefs. So I made the assumption clean blood—free of alcohol or unnecessary medications—was very important. I had no idea how I would accomplish this task at age seven; I just knew clean blood was significant. Water is one of your blood's best friends, as it flushes out the toxins. Throughout my entire life, I have never wavered from those beliefs. I also believe this to be one of the most important doctrines on health and slow aging. This belief has influenced many of my life decisions.

Clean Liver

Your blood must send the needed nutrients to detoxify, rebuild, and repair 300 billion cells a day. Never forget that your blood is a flowing chemical factory, feeding all your organs. Clean blood, a clean colon, and a clean liver contribute to a clean bill of health. Your liver is cleansed by drinking an adequate amount of water each day. According to Dr. Jeff Jones, your liver has more than 500 functions it must perform to clean your body's systems.

Give your liver the respect it deserves. Your liver is vital for protein production and for processing fats and sugars. Your liver is very happy when you exercise and only drink alcohol in limited amounts. Like your heart, you can't live without the functions the liver performs.

Common-Sense Anti-Aging Tips

* When washing, moisturizing, or applying makeup, work up and out. Fifty years of pulling down on your face and neck muscles will take its toll.
* Stained yellow teeth are extremely aging. Dental science has developed endless methods to keep teeth white for a beautiful smile.
* Using self-tanning lotion on legs and feet makes them appear more youthful.
* Tinted hair should always include highlights, as one solid color looks very unnatural.
* Dark hair colors are less flattering to an aging face. Lighter colors soften the age lines on the face.
* For hair spray buildup, mix baking soda (sodium bicarbonate) with your shampoo for your next hair wash.
* Overly permed hairstyles are aging. Go for a softer look.
* Color your roots often if you do not like gray hair.
* Wearing the same hairstyle you wore in your high school yearbook photo does not work anymore. You are no longer 17.

* Put a dab of cream-colored eye shadow on the corner of your eyes next to your nose.
* To soften laugh lines, use a lighter shade of foundation makeup on lines and under your eyes.
* Vitamin C stimulates collagen production when applied to your skin.
* Use a body wash in your bath or shower. Soap is drying.
* Exfoliate the skin often. I suggest Sensaria salt sea scrub for arms and legs.
* Moisturize heels and elbows daily.
* Before you get age spots, help prevent them by using sunscreen daily.
* Manicured nails and a beautiful piece of jewelry make hands appear younger. Too many rings, however, bring too much attention to aging hands.
* There comes a time in a woman's life when she should stop wearing sleeveless clothes.
* Paint your toenails in a bright color just for fun.
* Eat off a small plate to help with portion control.
* If lacking energy, eat foods rich in phosphorus, such as pinto beans.
* Caffeine and alcohol dehydrate the body and lead to toxin buildup. Limit your intake.
* Melt butter in a saucepan. Add an equal amount of extra virgin olive oil, stir, and refrigerate. Use on toast and vegetables.
* One piece of chocolate cake contains the equivalent of 16 sugar cubes. One cola contains 9 teaspoons of sugar.
* By age 50, you have lost 15 pounds of muscle mass—so lift those weights.
* To keep your legs strong, get up from chairs without using your hands for support.
* Power-breathe daily—your cells will be happy.
* Getting a regular massage often brings fresh nutrients to your cells, making it easier for them to create new collagen.
* Maintaining close relationships and an active social life can contribute to your youthfulness and happiness.

Let's Talk Food

Then God said, "I give you every seed-bearing plant on the face of the whole earth and every tree that has fruit with seed in it. They will be yours for food. And to all the beasts of the earth and all the birds of the air and all the creatures that move on the ground—everything that has the breath of life in it—I give every green plant for food." And it was so.

—Genesis 1:29–30 (NIV)

It's time to get honest. How many of you have outdated supplements in your cupboards? Chances are you were talked into buying the latest miracle pill from a friend who just signed with a multilevel sales company. From toe fungus to hair loss, these companies have all the answers to your problems—shop wisely.

For the first time in history, we are presently a middle-aged society. The spotlight on anti-aging and antioxidant products and foods has never burned brighter. The World Health Organization (WHO) estimates that four billion people, 80 percent of the world's population, presently use herbal medicine for some aspect of primary health care. We desire to stay young and healthy. Here is my take on supplements: use caution. Everything the human body needs can be found in the fruit, vegetable, grain, dairy, and meat aisles of your market. Grab a shopping cart and load up. When you buy a banana, what you get is a nutritious food that contains everything God intended for it to contain. When we eat processed foods, scientists are making the decisions on what our foods should contain.

Personally, I trust the Creator of the universe any day over a food scientist. A homemade cake has approximately eight ingredients, foods whose names you can pronounce. Baking powder, eggs, flour, oil, sugar, vanilla, salt, and milk are familiar items. Check a cake mix box, and you will find 25 ingredients. What we do not add is monocalcium phosphate or monohydrate, partially hydrogenated soybean oil or thiamin mononitrate. I believe we are living longer, healthier lives due to the advances in health and medical science, not food additives.

The three leading causes of death in the United States are coronary artery disease, cancer, and stroke. Diet is a significant factor in the risk of each of these diseases. Eliminate saturated, hydrogenated, and polyunsaturated fats. Focus your diet on God-designed foods.

When I was a child, I seldom heard the word *cancer*. It now seems like an epidemic, and it seems to be hitting younger and younger people. I am shocked by the number of young women in my Bible study group fighting breast cancer. Why?

Is it stress, deodorants, or chemically treated foods? I grew up in an era when the bulk of our diet consisted of whole, fresh God-created food. As I sit here munching on a health bar, I count 29 additives. If all this stuff is so good for us, why are we the most overweight nation on Earth? Are we really that out of control?

Junk food facts interest me. Americans eat 17 billion quarts of popcorn a year, six pounds of potato chips per person per year, and 12 million pounds a year of cheese for Cheetos. Ninety-eight percent of households in the United States keep ice cream in their freezer. One company alone supplies 200,000 servings of cheesecake to restaurants daily.

Two items, often considered junk food, that you can eat without feeling guilty (unless you are allergic) are peanuts and peanut butter. Peanuts are packed with vitamins A, E, and C, calcium, magnesium, potassium, and fiber. Eat one ounce of peanuts or two tablespoons of peanut butter daily. You will receive the benefit of as much fiber as a typical slice of whole wheat bread.

A quick warning: some experts suspect artificial sweeteners may actually stimulate your appetite; so forget the diet drinks. A study at the University of Texas at San Antonio found that people who drank a can or bottle of soda a day were 37 percent more likely to become overweight than those who did not drink any soda. One of my children's friends was completely hooked on diet cola. After her mother died young, she decided she had better take charge of her health. She gave up diet cola and quickly lost ten pounds.

Antioxidants: God's Diet for Anti-Aging and Health

With the aging of America, serious attention is paid to all antioxidant products. NBC's *Today* show reported that the Yanomami Indians of the Amazon Basin have believed for centuries that the Açaí Berry holds unique power, and anyone who eats or drinks this berry juice will have a burst of energy. Some medical professionals call this berry juice "super food" for age-defying beauty. The berry comes from the Brazilian rain forest and is touted as one of the most powerful antioxidants discovered to date. The berry has become a celebrity. From the *Oprah Winfrey Show* to *Vogue* magazine, it has been called "the next workout cocktail"—but don't jump in until all the facts are in.

Once I became educated on antioxidant foods I was hooked. To put it simply, antioxidants are nutrients that protect the body from damage caused by free radicals. Free radicals are produced when the body uses oxygen for energy and when your body is exposed to environmental toxins such as car exhaust, cigarette smoke, and other pollution. Free radicals attack molecules; the more free radicals, the more damage to your immune system. It is now believed this process is responsible for the body's decline as we age.

If you live in a heavily populated area, center your diet on antioxidants. The body is unable to repair the free radical damage fast enough. Our body's cells are undergoing a continuous cycle of oxidation, and we become subject to age-related degenerative diseases. When antioxidants are paired with other antioxidants, they are more effective. A, E, and C are the antioxidant vitamins. Zinc and selenium are mineral antioxidants.

To make antioxidant eating a habit, start with berries. Blueberries, strawberries, raspberries, and cranberries are rich in soluble fiber; so fill up on these delicious colorful fruits. Pomegranate juice is also a recent favorite of antioxidant-obsessed boomers. One 8-ounce glass a day can reverse cellular damage to the heart. When I was a child, V8 vegetable juice was a popular health drink. Today, it is advertised as an antioxidant, anti-aging drink and is experiencing renewed popularity with boomers. If you prefer not to eat your veggies, drink them! Just remember you are responsible for the care of those 60 trillion cells; so do your part and keep them happy.

My personal skin care diet revolves around nuts—especially almonds, peanuts, and walnuts—avocados, and fresh fruit. (My girls believe I could eat sawdust if it was served with an avocado.) I make antioxidant homemade spaghetti sauce with onions, garlic, olive oil, green peppers, whole tomatoes, tomato sauce, and spices, then I forego the pasta. Peanut butter with apples, celery, or bananas are my favorites, or a mashed avocado on multigrain toast, or even oatmeal with honey for breakfast, and chicken salad and vegetables for lunch. Just before bed, I enjoy sugarless gelatin to help rebuild bone. And remember—a full day's supply of water is 60 to 80 ounces.

Nutrients are what keep us alive. There are more than 50 different nutrients, chemicals, vitamins, minerals, and fatty and amino acids—and your body needs all of them. God put all 50 in the foods we eat; that is, *if* we eat a variety of foods. Center your diet with the following antioxidant, anti-aging, and skin-loving foods:

If your skin is dry, eat avocado, olive oil, and citrus, and drink your water. To help prevent wrinkles, eat food rich in vitamin C. For dull skin, there are skin brighteners available, but if you wish to go the natural way, foods containing vitamin A, such as dark green and orange vegetables, will help. For aging skin, eat broccoli, dark chocolate, and any other foods loaded with antioxidants. When stressed, try fish, curried dishes, and cucumbers.

In his love for his creation of humankind, God placed on this earth everything we need to survive, plus nature's beauty and wonders for our enjoyment and pleasure. Eliminate as many processed foods from your diet as possible. Know your young (good) fats from aging (bad) fats. For weight control, also limit your intake of baked goods, white rice, white bread, and other high-carb foods.

You and only you will dictate your health, body fitness, and face. Excessive amounts of coffee, black tea, alcohol, and processed sugar weaken your immune system. No matter how great a full day in the sun with a never-ending supply of margaritas sounds, it will put your skin on suicide watch. Don't kill your skin. Remember—it is holding you together.

Eat a spectrum of colorful, whole, live foods—foods that decay when they are too old to nourish your body. God's food spoils. In some cases, processed food can last for years. Just like our heavenly Father put color in flowers to attract the creatures of the air to a food source, he put color in our foods to attract us to the essential components that keep us healthy. Many researchers now believe antioxidants work only when they are in food. So forget the pills; eat vitamin-rich food.

Food of the Gods

Dark chocolate is good for our brain. It contains chemically active compounds that improve our mood by increasing serotonin and endorphins. Unfortunately, our brain shrinks as we age. With this knowledge, you can blame all your forgetfulness and mistakes on your shrinking brain.

Our brain is about 60 percent fats and must be fed properly. To keep your brain fit and healthy, exercise has been proven to be one of your brain's best medicines. If you exercise just 120 minutes (30 minutes a day, four days) a week, you can keep your brain two to three years younger. Exercise also retards the onset of Alzheimer's. (A new case of Alzheimer's is diagnosed in the United States every minute and 15 seconds.)

The botanical name for chocolate is *Theobroma cacao,* which appropriately translates to "food of the gods." If it is good for the gods, it has to be good for us mortals. The antioxidants in chocolate act like aspirin, thinning your blood. No more guilt. Eat that piece of dark chocolate with the knowledge you are enhancing blood flow, lowering your blood pressure, making your heart happy, and feeding your brain. You go, girl!

A serving of dark chocolate measures 9,000 units on the antioxidant activity scale, but unfortunately a serving is not the size of a giant Hershey bar. It is only 1.6 ounces (darn!). Dark chocolate has saturated fat, the kind that does not raise your cholesterol. This delicious super-antioxidant protects the body's cells, lowers bad cholesterol, and helps to prevent blood clotting and type II diabetes. More good news! Chocolate contains more flavonoids than twenty-three different vegetables. Eat your chocolate the same time you pop your vitamin pill. All this great news comes with this reminder, though: moderation in all things.

Blueberries and fish are two more foods that help delay the aging of your brain. Fish contains the essential fatty acids the brain needs to function properly. As I am not a fish lover, I prefer to get my fatty acids by eating avocadoes and taking fish oil capsules. Guacamole and chips, with a chaser of dark chocolate and a handful of blueberries—it's a good life!

Nature's Nectar

My son, eat thou honey, because it is good;
and the honeycomb, which is sweet to thy taste."
—PROVERBS 24:13

Bees are nature's sweet factory workers. How honey is produced is one of nature's miracles. Science has never been able to manufacture a genuine honey; only bees know the secret of honeymaking. The average hive contains about 50,000 bees. The bees must visit 2 million flowers to make one pound of this miraculous natural healer.

In the year 2400 BC, the Egyptians recognized honey as an essential natural cure-all. Honey is mentioned 500 times in 900 remedies in an ancient Egyptian medical document. Honey is the sweetest food in God's miracle medical garden.

Honey has become a staple ingredient in some of today's most sought after beauty products according to www.newbeauty.com. Honey is a natural humectant, meaning it attracts and retains moisture. It contains essential vitamins and is full of minerals such as zinc and magnesium, which increase the skin's moisture retention. Rich in antioxidants, honey helps regenerate damaged tissue. Bee pollen has been called nature's perfect food. It contains all eight essential amino acids. For information on honey skin products, go to www.smarter.com.

Before bed, take a cup of hot water, add two teaspoons of honey and two teaspoons of apple cider vinegar to help your digestive system run smoothly. It also helps promote weight loss. The Bible mentions honey numerous times throughout its text; take note of God's gift of honey for our health. If you need some quick energy, how about a spoonful of honey! Honey is the only food on Earth that never spoils.

Mother Was Right! Eat Your Breakfast

As we age, our number 1 priority is keeping our health. People are living longer lives, but who wants to live longer if you are not healthy? After your morning weigh-in, head to the kitchen for a nourishing breakfast to kick-start your metabolism. If you are not a coffee drinker but need a jump start, perhaps an energy drink will get you going. Since I don't drink either of these, my morning drink is hot water, honey, and two teaspoons of lemon juice. Try it for a week, you may like it.

I am also a big believer in oatmeal with walnuts, blueberries, or cinnamon for breakfast. Oatmeal has a positive effect on both your good and bad cholesterol, cinnamon lowers your blood sugar, and walnuts are great for the heart and skin, and for energy production. Regular oatmeal is a great source of insoluble fiber. Insoluble fiber has great cancer-fighting properties, and the fiber attacks certain bile acids, reducing their toxicity.

If you eat oats regularly, you are less likely to develop heart disease and a number of other health issues. Oats are a good source of many nutrients, including vitamin E, zinc, selenium, copper, iron, manganese, and magnesium. Oats are also a good source of protein. A little protein powder can make your oats a high-protein breakfast without the fat.

Worthy of Thought

Throughout Anti-Aging God's Way, I have addressed the mind, body, and soul. I believe an explanation of what I interpret the soul to be is justified here.

The soul is the spiritual part of a human being, the seat of your most deeply felt emotions. The soul is your central element. Your soul is what houses your conscience, and your heart houses your soul.

When someone injures your soul, you respond with feelings of resentment and/or deep emotional pain. Every time you feel emotionally devalued, you put a stone in a wall that separates you from the offender. The greater the hurt, the higher and wider the wall. When a person claims to have found her soul mate, she is stating that the person is sensitive to her feelings, that their philosophies are in unison with one another. The soul is where your emotions exist. It is your spiritual and moral force, your inner person, your inner compass.

Your character is not your soul, your character is the sum total of all your habits. However, it is the human soul that changes one's character.

People who believe in a spiritual soul believe life on Earth is a temporary assignment. Those who believe in Jesus have the security of knowing that their soul will live forever in Heaven.

Your body belongs to you. Your mind and intellect belong to the world. Your heart belongs to those you love, but *your soul belongs to God.*

Many, many years ago when my children needed a babysitter, I only had to go next door, where a 14-year-old girl lived. No one would have called this girl a beauty. She was short, overweight, and average in appearance. She was sweet, kind, gentle, and fun, but in my daughters' young eyes she was beautiful.

In God's flower garden, there are thousands of flowers. Is a rose more beautiful than a lily? Is a sunflower more beautiful than a tulip? Is a geranium more beautiful than an orchid? Who is to say? God's flower garden consists of many colors, forms, and sizes, and so it is with people.

Please remember there are people out there who think you are one of the most beautiful people they have ever seen. It upsets me to think there are women in the world who think of themselves as a weed or a thorn in God's garden. Every woman is a beautiful flower—different, actually unique, and special in her uniqueness. She is without equal. That is the way God sees you. His creation—a woman—is a being that creates new life. She is unmatched.

How I wish I could influence you to see how beautiful you truly are! Does the rose wilt because it sees an orchid? The rose does not compete with the orchid or compare itself with a gardenia. The rose just keeps being a rose. The lesson here? Never compare yourself with another. When you start the comparison game, you will always lose. Do not compare your negatives to other women's positives. The rose does not dwell on its thorns but simply goes on to produce a beautiful flower. Take a lesson from nature, and just be the best you can be. Be who you really are, your true self. Self-esteem is a key ingredient to anti-aging. The feeling that you are worthy of self-esteem simply implies the value you place on who you are as a person, your ideas, your feelings, your desires, and your dreams.

Of all the people who have walked on this earth, no one has my thumb-print or yours; no one is exactly like me or you. No one loves exactly the same people I love or you love; no one has had exactly the same experiences as I have or you have. I know that to compare yourself to others is to under-mine your own worth and value. We are all very unique. We are alike, yet so different. The one constant in our lives that unites and connects us is that God loves us equally. He loves me as much as he loves the person who can donate one million dollars to his church or charity.

I love what age has taught me about risk! If you want to live life to the fullest, take a chance. I value deeply what I have learned through the decades; without love, we have not truly lived. Age has taught me that two of a person's strongest emotional needs are to feel important and to feel appreciated. Life has taught me to never give up on family, and to never let family or friends slip through your fingers, because once you do, you may not get them back.

My experiences have taught me that if I am serious about anti-aging, my life must be balanced. Balanced between mind, body, soul, work, family, play, and self. Most of all I have learned the power of love—God's love and humankind's love.

Determine to become one of the best. Maximize your abilities, make good decisions, form good habits, and do what you know you should, and you will achieve success. In 1 Corinthians, we read that God will never let us down; he will never let us be pushed past our limit; he'll always be there to help if we allow him (10:13). God's way of saving your face is for you to leave your problems in God's lap. I am still not all I should be, but I am bringing all my energies to bear on this one thing.

> *Forgetting the past and*
> *looking forward to what lies ahead.*
> **—PHILIPPIANS 3:13**

Life 101: What We Want vs. What We Need

What we *want* is a great job. . . . What we *need* is approval for a job well done.

What we *want* is to be rich . . . . What we *need* is to be loved

What we *want* is success in business . . . . What we *need* is success at home

What we *want* is to be heard . . . . What we *need* is to be believed

What we *want* is physical fulfillment. . What we *need* is emotional fulfillment

What we *want* is a beautiful face . . . . What we *need* is a beautiful heart

What we *want* is to achieve greatness. . . . . What we *need* is peace of mind

What we *want* is acknowledgment. . . . . .What we *need* is acceptance

What we *want* is to have great sex . . . . .What we *need* is abiding love

What we *want* is to know important people . . . What we *need* are true friends

What we *want* is everything. . . . . What we *need* is God

—BOBBIE GEE

Words of Inspiration

❋ The body is the servant of the mind.

❋ But Christ, God's faithful Son, is in complete charge of God's house. And we Christians are God's house—he lives in us! (Hebrews 3:6)

❋ A beautiful woman lacking discretion and modesty is like a fine gold ring in a pig's snout. (Proverbs 11:22)

❋ The only successful way to destroy a negative emotion is to verbalize a positive statement.

❋ White hair is a crown of glory and is seen most among the godly. (Proverbs 16:31)

❋ If anyone can control his tongue, it proves that he has perfect control over himself in every other way. (James 3:2)

❋ Kind words are like honey—enjoyable and healthful. (Proverbs 16:24)

❋ You must love and help your neighbors just as much as you love and take care of yourself. (James 2:8)

❋ For God has said, "I will never, *never* fail you nor forsake you." That is why we can say without any doubt or fear, "The Lord is my Helper and I am not afraid of anything that mere man can do to me." (Hebrews 13:5)

❋ Faith, the confident assurance that something you want to happen is going to happen. It is the certainty that what you hope for is waiting for you, even though you cannot see it.

❋ Faith is believing.

❋ Don't worry about anything . . . pray about everything . . . you will experience God's peace. (Philippians 4:6–7)

❋ Forgetting the past and looking forward to what lies ahead. (Philippians 3:13)

❋ Don't live to make a good impression on others. Be humble, thinking of others as better than yourself. (Philippians 2:3)

* How you feel determines your behavior more than what you know.
* Don't just be interested in and thinking of your own interest, but be interested in others in what they are doing. Your attitude should always be kind.
* A relaxed attitude lengthens a man's life; jealousy rots it away. (Proverbs 14:30)
* For the Holy Spirit, God's gift, does not want you to be afraid of people, but to be wise and strong, and to love them and enjoy being with them. If you will stir up this inner power, you will never be afraid to tell others about our Lord. (2 Timothy 1:7)
* Keep a close watch on all you do and think. (1 Timothy 4:16)
* Encourage one another daily. (Hebrews 3:13 NIV)
* A heart at peace gives life to the body, but envy rots the bones. (Proverbs 14:30 NIV)
* Always keep your conscience , doing what you know is right. (1 Timothy 1:19)
* The secret to successful aging is to maintain a healthy balance between your emotional and logical powers, along with your drive, desire, and persistence.
* You are the product of your choices.
* Realize your daily conversation is the automatic readout of your thoughts and subconscious emotions.
* Self-discipline is a learned pattern of behavior. It is a daily choice, and this develops into a lifestyle.
* The peacefulness of your mind will be a vital link to your anti-aging success story.
* In everything you do, put God first, and he will crown your efforts with success.
* Man's mind, once stretched by a new idea, never regains its original dimensions. (Oliver W. Holmes)

Part Five

COSMETIC
PROCEDURES

A Quick Word About Cosmetic Procedures

As we move on, with the understanding that lasting beauty comes from one's core beliefs, unselfish actions of serving others, and caring for ourselves, let's look at the advancements in medicine. I sincerely believe God has no problem with you making the most of what nature gave you, as long as you do not become addicted or obsessed.

It would be an exceptional world if we lived in a society where decisions concerning an individual were based on heart and character. In this no-time, must-hurry, gotta-go, nonperfect world we live in, it takes time to determine the condition of one's temperament, sincerity, and character.

Visiting a plastic surgeon, dermatologist, or skin care specialist has gone mainstream. After years of dedicated skin care and allegiance to topicals, I still was not satisfied with my skin texture.

Having had oily skin most of my life, I had clogged pores that robbed my skin of a smooth texture. I had never visited a dermatologist but made an appointment. With only two visits the results were dramatic. Whether for your skin's beauty or for its health, an annual visit with your dermatologist is as important as your yearly physical. Remember—skin cancer can kill.

If you believe, as did the farmer in his field, that God's handiwork could use a helping hand, following are a few of the medical or cosmetic choices you might consider. There are so many treatments available these days. So many, in fact, it can become confusing. Therefore, make sure you are working with a professional in the field of skin rejuvenation.

To help you understand the treatments available I contacted Shien-Lin

Garrett, PA-C*, B.S., M.S. Shien-Lin holds a master's degree in dermatology and is highly regarded by her patients in the area of skin health and rejuvenation. In 1999, she made the University of Southern California dean's list and for the past eight years, she has been the physician's assistant to Dr. Edward Kramer. Their offices are located in Anaheim and Laguna Niguel, California.

Shien-Lin Garrett, PA-C, B.S., M.S.

A beautiful woman in her late 40s came into my office two weeks before her wedding. Just six months earlier, in the middle of planning her wedding, she had been diagnosed with breast cancer. In addition to skin rejuvenation, she needed her spirits lifted to rid her of that stressed, tired look.

I suggested a fotofacial, Botox, and Restylane. After a short 30 minutes, we were finished. She looked at the results and began to cry. She said, "I look beautiful. I haven't looked like myself in six months; now I am me again, thank you so much." And on her wedding day, she looked beautiful.

Regularly, I see women with beautiful souls who have lost a little confidence due to aging, but with a few simple cosmetic procedures, the light in their eyes shines once again. The smiles on their faces make my work very gratifying. With the wide array of dermatological and cosmetic treatments available today, you can remove or improve many of the effects of long-term aging. You will look younger and more engaging.

Work with a professional you will feel confident in when choosing the skin rejuvenation treatment that is right for you. Start slow with non-invasive procedures. If the less invasive procedures do not give you the results you desire, you may choose to move to the more invasive procedures such as a mini-face-lift or Lifestyle Lift. With skin care, it is easier to prevent and preserve than to turn back the clock, but if you desire quick results, surgical procedures may be your only option. Always consider this before choosing surgery, though: surgical procedures can result in scarring *that may or may not be visible.*

---

* Physician Assistant Certified Fellow, Society of Dermatology Physician Assistants

The least invasive method for improving the appearance and preventing wrinkles is with topical creams, lotions, gels, and serums.

The three simplest things you can do to prevent sun damage and aging of your skin topically are sunscreens and sunblock every morning and a retin-A type topical cream at night.

Topicals

Topicals are the least invasive method of anti-aging. However, they will not give you the fastest results. You should, however, be on topicals in your maintenance regime at home, and then when combining other procedures or treatments, you will get great results. With so many products on the market, you must find products that work for you. Everyday changes in weather, hormones, and activities affect your skin's needs; so you may have to rotate among a few different topicals.

Vitamin A

Vitamin A derivatives are some of the best topicals you can use. They repair damage from the sun, help with brown spots and wrinkles, decrease pore size, shrink oil glands, and increase collagen in the skin. They help to remove or reduce the appearance of scars, and they clear and control acne. These include Retin-A, Tazorac, Retino, and Tretinion.

Depending on the strength and how often you apply these topicals, you may get some peeling and redness. Your skin, however, will get used to the products over time. I recommend you start by using them every third or fourth night for a month, then slowly increase to every other night and, if your skin is strong enough, every night.

AHAs

AHAs (alpha-hydroxy acids): glycolic acid, salicylic acid, and lactic acid.

Acids work by removing layers of the skin. The degree of improvement from an acid depends on how deep into the skin the acid peels. Products containing these ingredients help with improving fine lines, acne, brown spots, uneven color in the skin, increasing collagen, removing abnormal skin cells, improving texture, and dissolving dirt and old skin cells within the pores. Using any product containing these ingredients will result in skin that will be sensitive to the sun; therefore, a sunblock should be used alone every day and reapplied as needed.

Alpha-hydroxy acids (AHAs) may be used alone or in combination with a vitamin-A type derivative to treat mildly damaged skin. AHAs are derived from fruit and dairy products.

Peptides

Proteins are made up of smaller units called polypeptides. So basically a peptide is the building block for proteins found in the body.

Peptides repair skin cell integrity, promote formation of collagen and elastin, improve circulation, help with topical bacterial infections, support cellular health, hydrate the skin, and prevent inflammation. Inflammation is the basis for all aging. The nice thing about peptides is they do not cause peeling or redness, sun damage, or dark circles under the eyes. They decrease swelling and bruising associated with injections.

Antioxidants

Topical antioxidants, (especially vitamins A, C, and E), function to help cells repair damage caused by ultraviolet radiation and smoking. Newer products are now harnessing the antioxidant properties in plants and fruits to help protect the skin from the environment. These include the coffee berry, green tea, white tea, soybeans, pomegranate, sea kelp, grapes, micro-algae, rose and pink bark. Other antioxidants include idebenone, some flavonoids, coenzyme Q10, carotenes, lycopene, lipoic acid, astaxanthin, sirtuins, and some polyphenols.

The issue with topicals is getting the active ingredients deep enough into the skin to work. Most products need help to penetrate deeper into the skin to be of greater benefit. I recommend three different ways to increase the benefits from your topicals:

1. Clairsonic—It is a facial/body brush that uses ultrasonic waves to gently clean your skin; it also allows your products to penetrate 61 percent deeper into your skin. There are two different brushes for the same price of $195. One can be purchased over the counter and is not as strong as the one you can buy from your health care professional. I recommend the stronger one.

Stem cells. Any type of cell found in the body can be created from a stem cell. There are several companies who have stem cells in their products that help to regenerate your own skin. These products can help to heal your skin faster after chemical peels, laser treatments, and surgical procedures.

2. Rollcit—A home roller device with little, short needles that create small, painless channels into the deeper layers of the skin for your topicals to pass through.

3. Other topicals that removes skin cells. Using anything such as scrubs, Retin-A-like products, AHAs, or micro-dermabrasion, before applying your products will allow them to penetrate deeper and to work faster. Be cautious not to irritate your skin—do not overscrub or apply products that are overly irritating.

Moisturizers
Look for the following ingredients in a moisturizer. These ingredients are best for bringing moisture into and onto the skin.

1. Hyaluronic Acid (Sodium Hyaluronate)
2. Ceramides
3. Squalane
4. Nut butters and oils such as macadamia, shea, sunflower, and almond
5. Panthenol
6. Dimethicone

Injections

If considering injections, I advise taking Arnica Montana or Bromelain one day before any procedure that may cause bruising or swelling and to continue until swelling and bruising is gone (usually one to seven days). In my practice, the most satisfying procedures for my patients are Intense Pulsed light, Botox, and fillers. Combining all three can give you an amazing transformation without making you unrecognizable to your friends.

Botox

Botox is one of the favorite and most cost-effective procedures to help prevent wrinkles from becoming permanent. By eliminating "worry lines," "frown lines," crow's feet, and forehead lines you will appear rejuvenated. Botox may also be used to treat "smoker lines," as well as lines and bands in the neck.

A small needle is used to inject a purified protein into specific muscles in your face and neck to relax the muscles. The muscle can no longer make the motion that created the wrinkle in the first place.

The effects last three to six months depending on the dose injected. Botox has also proven effective for eliminating migraines and tension headaches. A word to the wise—one famous female designer is so full of Botox her face has become almost expressionless; so "Moderation in all things" continues to be the best motto.

No anesthetic is required, but if a topical anesthetic is used, the procedure can be painless. The procedure takes 5 to 20 minutes. The effects will be noticed in 2 to 10 days. Over time, the muscles become smaller, so subsequent injections last longer. Typically, there is no down time except for a small bump where the Botox is injected but is usually gone within 20 minutes. Side effects are bruising at the site of injection and less than 1 percent chance of droopy upper eyelid, which typically lasts about 4 weeks and will completely heal. Botox is very safe, and no one has been found to be allergic to it when used for cosmetic procedures. Botox was first used in children at much higher doses to treat muscle spasm due to cerebral palsy with positive effects. Botulism toxin treatment may be used in combination with other procedures for facial rejuvenation to achieve a more satisfying and lasting effect.

Dysport

Dysport is a new injectable product that has been used in Europe for years and is now available here in the United States. It is similar to Botox in its effect and use for anti-aging. Both Botox and Dysport are botulinum type A derivatives that relax the muscles that create dynamic wrinkles. Both Dysport and Botox are used to treat and prevent frown lines, crow's feet, forehead, and neck and lip lines. The units used are different, though. Approximately 3 Dysport units equal 1 unit of Botox. In my practice I've noticed a slightly faster onset of relaxation of the muscles with Dysport but ultimately both reach complete relaxation in about 2–10 days after injection. Both products last the same amount of time, approximately 3–5 months. Both products are about the same price, and both companies have frequent rebate programs to make the injections more affordable. Each person is unique, and the effects will differ in each person and is completely dependent on the practitioner injecting the patient.

Fillers

The dermal filler market has many product choices: collagen, Restylane, Perlane, Juvederm, Captique, Artefill, and Radesse, just to name a few. Fillers are wonderful for an immediate improvement for almost any wrinkle. There are thin fillers for superficial lines and thick fillers for the deep folds from your nose to the corners of your mouth. Most people prefer a non-invasive solution for the aging skin of the face; therefore, injectables are preferred. A substance that is compatible with your body is injected under the skin to lift up irregularities such as wrinkles, pits, and scars.

Collagen

Collagen is a protein substance found in all human and animal tissue. Most of the collagen used for soft-tissue augmentation is derived from cattle. However, for people who are allergic to bovine (cow-derived) products, collagen or collagen-related substances may be self-donated by the patient or obtained from a tissue donor. Your doctor will test you prior to collagen injection to determine if you are allergic to bovine collagen. Collagen injections are usually given in a series of treatments, until the desired effect of "filling out" a wrinkle or depression is achieved. A local anesthetic minimizes discomfort from the injection needle. The effects of the collagen injection may last for 3 to 12 months.

Prevelle Silk

Prevelle Silk is a soft-tissue filler made of hyaluronic acid and contains the local anesthetic lidocaine. Prevelle is injected into facial skin to treat moderate to severe wrinkles. The main advantage of this filler is that injections are less painful than other hyaluronic acid products because it is premixed with anesthetic. Prevelle Silk results last three to four months.

Side effects of Prevelle Silk include temporary injection site reactions such as swelling, pain/tenderness, redness, and lumps or bumps that last one to four days. Prevelle Silk costs about $400 for a .075-milliliter (ml) syringe.

Hylaform

Hylaform is a gel made of hyaluronic acid that allows quick, easy, and immediate corrections without the need for a skin test. It is injected just under the skin's surface at intervals along the wrinkle until the right amount is achieved. Hylaform gel can be used to "fill" and smooth out deep facial furrows, acne scars, and smile lines. It can also be used to enhance the lips.

Captique

Captique is a gel that contains a purified form of hyaluronic acid made from rooster combs. Since hyaluronic acid is a naturally occurring substance found in the body, pre-testing for sensitivity to the product is not necessary.

Like other fillers, Captique smooths facial lines and wrinkles. It can be used to treat different areas of the face, including crow's feet, nasolabial folds (smile lines), vertical lip lines, and "marionette" lines (lip corners). Results last approximately four to six months.

Restylane

Restylane is a dermal filler made of a crystal-clear gel from a non-clear gel from a non-animal source. Hyaluronic acid is used to treat lines around the eyes, lips, cheeks, forehead, and smile lines. It can be used to lift the eyebrow, rejuvenate the hands, and fill in depressed or sunken scars. Restylane is biodegradable and completely biocompatible with your body. Restylane lasts about six months.

Perlane

Perlane is thicker, longer-lasting hyaluronic acid filler made by the same company as Restylane and is used to fill deeper folds of the face, enhance lips, and add volume to the face. It usually lasts about 12 months.

Juvederm Ultra and Juvederm Ultra Plus

Juvederm Ultra and Juvederm Ultra Plus are non-animal forms of hyaluronic acid gel, a naturally occurring substance that binds water to cells. Since this category of filler is not derived from an animal source, allergic reactions are rare. Juvederm is injected to fill out folds and lines. The most common areas to have injected are lips, lines between the nose and mouth, smile lines, and downward corners of the mouth. Results last five to eight months for the Juvederm Ultra and approximately 12 months for the Juvederm Ultra Plus. Juvederm is similar to Restylane; however, it lasts approximately 20 percent longer. With all hyaluronic-based fillers, serious side effects are rare. Temporary bruising and swelling lasting 24 to 48 hours occurs in some patients. An anesthetic block is done prior to the procedure to decrease the possibility of bruising and pain.

Fat Transfers

Fat transfer is the process of harvesting body fat from the patient's own body, then injecting it to replace fat lost from under the skin in the aging process. Defects improved by fat injections include creases around the nose, mouth, and chin, and the sunken appearance and "drawn look" under the eyes created by loss of fat pads in the cheeks. The improvements in appearance vary between patients. Fat is not helpful for fine lines because it is too thick. Some follow-up treatments may be necessary. This procedure is performed on an outpatient basis. If you are having liposuction anyway, it would be great to transfer the fat removed to other areas that need it. It is not possible to be allergic to your own fat, and it can last six months to several years. In some cases, a permanent improvement results.

Radiesse

Radiesse is a relatively new injectable product used in a variety of applications. Its primary advantages are its potential for long-lasting effect and its ability to stimulate collagen formation. Radiesse does not require allergy testing.

Radiesse can be injected into facial folds and lines, depressed scars, or other areas needing cosmetic correction. Its longevity is usually 12 to 18 months depending on the area treated and the metabolism of the person being treated. This product is FDA-approved for facial aesthetic contouring.

Sculptra (New-Fill)

As we age, we lose fat in our face. Sculptra (or New-Fill outside the United States) can treat facial fat loss that results in sunken cheeks, indentations, and hollow eyes. It can also be used to fill in deep smile lines. Sculptra is a safe, synthetic, and biocompatible material injected below the surface of the skin in the area of fat loss. It provides a gradual and significant increase in skin thickness, improving the appearance of folds and sunken areas. No skin testing is required. Sculptra lasts for 18 to 24 months. Several (three to six) injection sessions are required to achieve the final correction.

Artefill

Artefill is a unique combination of a collagen gel, tiny synthetic beads, and an anesthetic agent. It is used to treat the deep smile lines that run from your nose to the corners of your mouth. A skin test is done 28 days before your first injection. If you are allergic to collagen you cannot use this product. If you are not allergic you may begin your series of injections (usually two or three sessions are needed to give you the look you want). A small needle is used to inject the filler and usually only a topical anesthetic is needed to control discomfort. Artefill contains very tiny, round, smooth, non-reabsorbable beads of polymehtymethacrylate that are carried in a collagen gel that immediately fills in the area injected, giving you an instantaneous result. As your body absorbs the injected collagen, your own collagen takes its place. Because Artefill is not reabsorbed by your body, it should be injected in stages by an Artefill-trained practitioner over a period of several weeks to months. Artefill fills the gaps, raising the skin to its normal height. Over time (two to three months), your body will permanently surround the Artefill for a long-lasting effect. It takes about three months for the full effect to be seen. The procedure lasts 5 to 20 minutes.

Silicone

In 1998, an independent National Science Panel reported silicone to be safe. Silicone oil is injected in very small droplets, through a tiny needle at multiple points under the skin, to treat lines around the mouth, frown lines, depressed scars, crow's feet, and smile lines (nasolabial fold), and to enhance the lips. Over time, skin cells produce new collagen, which in turn grows around the silicone droplets. More collagen growth is stimulated by continued injections, spread over time. As this progression continues, the collagen-encapsulated silicone droplets gradually fill in the depression or wrinkle. Typically treatments are spread over several months. The number of treatments required will vary depending on how deep or long the defect.

The results are gradual; you will notice more improvement with each session. As full correction approaches, injections can be expanded to three- to six-month intervals. A local anesthetic may be used to reduce the discomfort during the injections. Silicone is considered a permanent filler.

Effectiveness of Fillers

Filler*	Lasts
Collagen	2–4 months
Cosmoplast	2–4 months
Hylaform	3 months
Hylaform Plus	3–6 months
Captique	4–6 months
Restylane	6–12 months
Perlane	12 months or longer
Juvederm Ultra	6–12 months
Juvederm Ultra Plus	12 months or longer
Fat Transfer	1–2 years
Radiance	2–7 years
Sculptra (New-Fill)	18 months–2 years
Dermalive	permanent
Autograft	permanent
Allograft	permanent
Silicone	permanent
Artefill	permanent

*All are FDA-approved

With any injectable wrinkle filler, local swelling or redness may occur immediately following treatment and is temporary. This will subside within a few days. Occasional bruises at the injection site can occur, which can be covered with makeup. Any discomfort following the procedure can be controlled with medication. Rare problems that may be persistent include lumpiness, or granulomas. These conditions are easily treated by your physician. This issue typically occurs with the longer-lasting fillers versus temporary fillers.

Laser Skin–Tightening Systems

While Polaris and Titan are the laser skin-tightening systems most recognized by patients, there are a variety of systems available, including ReFirme, LuxIR, and Aluma. Each is specifically designed to offer unique benefits and results, so one system may be better suited to a particular patient's needs than another's. Learn about the different laser skin-tightening systems available.

DocShop.com can help you *find a cosmetic dermatologist* in your area today.

Titan Skin-Tightening

The Titan skin-tightening system is a revolutionary technology that tones, lifts, and tightens skin by stimulating the rebuilding of collagen under the skin's surface. Titan is safe for skin-tightening on all parts of the body. Titan skin-tightening is also a very effective treatment for loose and wrinkled skin on the neck.

The Titan system uses infrared (laser) energy delivered through the sapphire tip of a handheld device to tighten the skin comfortably and safely. As the Titan laser skin-tightening device is applied to the skin, a six-second cooling and heating cycle treats dime-sized areas, heating the collagen below the skin. The laser is applied to the skin multiple times. The face and neck can be treated within an hour. No anesthesia is necessary and there is no downtime or recovery period. Tighter, more toned skin is usually noted after the first Titan treatment, and the skin-tightening continues over the next few months as collagen growth continues. Best results are often obtained by undergoing two laser skin-tightening treatment sessions about a month apart. Most patients enjoy the results of Titan laser skin-tightening for up to two years; however, results can be maintained with touch-up sessions.

Polaris Skin-Tightening

The Polaris skin-tightening system is FDA-approved technology used to treat wrinkles on the face, including crow's feet and wrinkles around the mouth. What sets Polaris apart from other laser skin-tightening technology is that it uses a combination of laser energy and radio frequency (RF) energy. These two energies work together to provide more effective treatment and increased patient comfort.

The laser energy from the Polaris system treats the wrinkles at the skin's surface and improves the skin tone. The RF energy heats the deeper tissues, promoting new collagen formation, treating deeper wrinkles, and producing a skin-tightening effect. The heat produced by the Polaris laser is specifically calculated to deliver the most beneficial heat possible deep into the patient's dermis. Polaris produces enough heat to cause lax tissues to contract and induce collagen production, yet not enough heat to harm or burn the skin. The best candidates for Polaris skin-tightening have mild to moderate facial and or/neck wrinkles, and thin or moderately thick skin. Most patients who undergo Polaris skin-tightening will benefit most from four to five treatments a few weeks apart. Polaris skin-tightening is reported to be more comfortable than Thermage, which uses only RF energy.

Refirme Skin-Tightening

The Refirme skin-tightening system is unique in that it uses lower levels of energy, which results in increased patient comfort. With a more rapid pulse repetition rate (one pulse per second) than other systems, the Refirme system also means faster treatment for patients and less fatigue for operators. In addition to producing excellent results for the face and neck, the Refirme skin-tightening system is highly effective for treating other areas of the body, including the legs, arms, abdomen, and buttocks.

Aluma Skin-Tightening

Like other systems, the Aluma skin-tightening system uses a laser that bypasses the epidermis, which means no post-procedure downtime for patients. A touch screen and intuitive operating system makes the Aluma method simple for practioners to use, which means they can focus on patient comfort and results. The Aluma skin-tightening system handpiece is ergonomically designed to provide superior accuracy and ease of use, which means more precise results for the patient. Aluma uses a vacuum system to isolate the exact target area to be treated, producing highly predictable and effective results and eliminating the risk of affecting surrounding tissues.

LuxIR Skin-Tightening

The LuxIR is a laser skin-tightening system unique because of its handpiece and application method. With LuxIR, as with other systems, the laser beam reaches from 1.5 mm to 3.0 mm into the dermis, but bypasses the epidermis layer to reduce damage to the skin. LuxIR is unique because of its handpiece, which has a safety mechanism that prevents laser pulses from beginning until the full handpiece surface is in contact with the patient's skin. This contact sensor prevents uneven heating, which could damage the skin, detracting from the rejuvenating effects of the treatment.

Another key feature of the LuxIR skin-tightening system is the one-of-a-kind handpiece head, which creates a network of tiny islets that are affected by the laser, while the surrounding areas remain untouched. This allows for the collagen growth stimulated in areas affected by the lasers to be supplemented with the patient's existing collagen from the undamaged area.

Dermatological Procedures

Thermage

Thermage uses radio waves to gently heat the skin. There is no downtime with Thermage. Slight swelling can occur with higher levels of energy, but usually, it is only the patient who can see the swelling. Thermage is used to lift and tighten the skin on the face or anywhere else on the body. Results vary from person to person, so the degree of improvement depends on the patient, the medical staff doing the procedure, and the number of sessions done to the area. Results can be immediate but are more likely to occur within the 12 months following the procedure. Discomfort during the procedure can range from 0 to 10 on a scale of 10, depending on the energy used, location being treated, and whether pain medication was used before treatment.

IPL (Intense Pulsed Light) / Fotofacial

IPLs, or fotofacials, are very popular with the majority of people because they have minimal downtime and great results. IPLs use visible light enhanced and filtered by a crystal that is placed on the skin to improve brown spots, redness, rosacea, broken capillaries, pore size, and skin texture; and to tighten the skin. Before the treatment, a clear gel is placed on the skin to conduct the light into the skin. The specific wavelengths of light heat the water in red and brown areas found in the skin, causing redness to fade over a few weeks, the brown spots to peel off within a week, and collagen production to be stimulated over the next few months. FotoFacial Aurora by Syneron utilizes a combination of intense light and RF energy. Aurora is able to offer a safe, non-invasive treatment for skin rejuvenation of one's face and body. Treatments will significantly improve sun damage, brown spots, rosacea, broken capillaries, pore size, and skin texture, and tightens the skin and reduces wrinkles with essentially no downtime.

Levulan Photodynamic Therapy

Photodynamic therapy (PDT) is a treatment preformed with a topical agent called Levulan (5-aminolevulinic acid or ALA) that makes your skin more sensitive to light. It is activated by the correct wavelength of light from either a blue light or IPL (intense pulsed light).

These treatments remove sun-damaged, precancerous zones, fine lines, and blotchy pigmentation, and minimize pores and reduce oil glands, effectively treating stubborn acne vulgaris, acne rosacea, and sebaceous hyperplasia, improving skin texture and the appearance of some acne scars.

For the best results, people usually have two or three treatments. You may need a treatment every two to four weeks. The treated areas can appear red and swollen with some peeling for two to seven days. Some patients have an exuberant response to PDT and experience marked redness of their skin. Temporary swelling of the lips and around the eyes can occur for a few days. Darker-pigmented patches called liver spots can become temporarily darker and then peel off, leaving normal skin. (This usually occurs over 7 to 10 days). Repeat treatments may be necessary. Levulan improves the whole facial area treated, creating one color, texture, and tone rather than just treating with liquid nitrogen, cautery, and surgery.

Chemical Peels

Chemical peels rejuvenate the skin by improving fine wrinkles, blemishes, uneven skin pigmentation, and acne. Chemical peels exfoliate the superficial dead skin layers and stimulate collagen production. A few days following the procedure, you will not want to be seen by anyone except your closest allies, as your skin will become dry, dark, and start to peel off over a period of days. If you make a public appearance, you are a very brave woman.

Chemical peeling is effective only for surface skin damage. Chemical peels are wonderful for removing abnormal skin cells, brown spots, pre-cancers, and wrinkles; reducing pore size; and improving the appearance of acne scarring/skin and chickenpox scarring. The amount of improvement given by peels depends on how many layers of skin are removed at the time of treatment and how many peels a person has done. I recommend having a series of three to five peels, one every two to four weeks. You will see improvement in your skin after each treatment.

No sedation or anesthetic is required; however, depending on the strength and type of peels, it can feel like hot chili sauce on your face for 5 to 10 minutes. The procedure lasts 20 to 30 minutes. Flaking and/or peeling will occur several days following the procedure. Patients may prefer a series of light peels to achieve their desired results, thereby decreasing the amount of peeling and/or flaking; sun avoidance is important.

Patients with olive or darker skin types may undergo light peels without difficulty; however, deeper peels can cause uneven darkening of the skin in people with darker skin and should be avoided unless the doctor decides it is safe.

In chemical peel treatment, a chemical solution is applied to facial skin, causing the skin to become dry and dark, and peel off over a period of days. As the treated skin peels, new skin forms to take its place.

A mild chemical peel is usually all that is necessary to treat fine lines and wrinkles around the eyes and mouth. Patients with minimum skin damage often respond best to a series of light peels in combination with a skin care program that includes retinoids and a sunscreen protection program. A medium-depth peel is often more effective for patients with moderate skin damage, including age spots, freckles, and actinic keratoses. A medium-depth peel may be combined with another treatment, such as laser resurfacing, to achieve maximum effectiveness.

The immediate aftereffect of a chemical peel is similar to sunburn. After a mild or superficial peel, redness and scaling of the skin may last three to five days. Medium-depth or deep peeling can result in redness, swelling, blistering, and peeling for 7 to 14 days. Medications are prescribed to alleviate discomfort.

Overexposure to sun must be avoided for a period of time to prevent sun damage, as the new skin is susceptible to injury. Chemical peeling is effective only on surface skin damage. The most common peeling agents are lactic acid, glycolic acid, vitamin A, Phenol, Jessner's Peel Solution, recorcinol, trichloroacetic acid, and carbolic acid.

Plasma Resurfacing

Plasma is one of the newest technologies for skin rejuvenation therapy. Plasma resurfacing tightens the skin, removes benign skin lesions, and improves skin discoloration, all with minimal downtime. There is no laser, just excited nitrogen particles.

Portrait skin regeneration, which uses nitrogen plasma energy, is unique in that it is the first and only technology proved to alter the structure of skin below the surface. This creates a long-lasting effect that improves wrinkles, tone, texture, and discoloration of the skin. Portrait is clinically proven to create exceptional conditions for the continual regeneration of skin and has been found to show improvements for as long as a year after treatment. The procedure is performed with topical anesthesia and minimal sedation because it can be painful. Areas typically treated are the face, neck, chest, and hands.

Lasers

Lasers work well by being attracted to different colors. Each laser is different and provides treatment for different conditions. When the laser light flashes onto the skin, it will heat up whatever it is attracted to. If it is attracted to water, it will heat the water in the skin and stimulate the growth of collagen, which will help the skin look tighter and smoother. If the laser is attracted to colors in the skin, it will cause the spots to heat up and either fade instantly or, over time, darken and scab, then peel off.

Laser Skin-Resurfacing

Lasers are used to remove or improve wrinkles, lines, and other effects of aging, sun damage, scars, red growths, brown spots, melasma, tattoos, warts, unwanted hair, and some skin cancers. Lasers can also treat deep-pigmented lesions such as port wine stains and birthmarks. The laser (light amplification by stimulated emission of radiation) is a "light pump." Lasers are powerful instruments, and laser surgery should be performed only by a practitioner with experience in the procedure.

Facial Laser-Resurfacing

Facial laser resurfacing is a technology specifically designed to eliminate superficial and moderately deep wrinkles of the face, moderate acne scarring, and sun-damaged skin. The laser-resurfacing works by precisely removing the top layer of skin. This removes the extra fold, which is causing the wrinkle, leaving a normal skin surface. Laser resurfacing also affects the collagen in the skin by heating the collagen, which promotes new collagen formation, and tightens the skin to give it a more uniform and smooth appearance. There can be significant downtime and healing with this procedure depending on the laser and energy used. In my experience with lasers, usually the more downtime you have, the better the results. If you are a person who wants to get the best results in one treatment with a laser, you should expect to hide from the world for about 7 to 10 days and wear makeup to hide the redness for 2 to 12 months. With the lasers that can provide no downtime to minimal downtime, you typically require multiple treatments, and it can take months before the ultimate result is achieved.

There are several different types of laser treatments: Fraxel, Profractional, Affirm, Erbium, Vbeam, Iriderm, Active FX CO2, Max CO2. Talk to your skin care provider as to which one best suits your needs. Most lasers tighten the skin and smooth wrinkles. Laser treatments can remove brown spots, sun damage, birthmarks, spider veins, and tattoos, and improve scarring.

Fractional Laser-Resurfacing

Fractional resurfacing is a cosmetic treatment that employs a laser to remove wrinkles, reduce acne scarring, alleviate dark pigmentation, and improve other conditions of the skin. Unlike earlier laser technologies, with fractional resurfacing, only a tiny proportion of the skin receives the laser light. The laser delivers a series of microscopic, closely spaced laser spots to the skin, while preserving the normal, healthy skin between. This preservation of healthy skin results in rapid healing following the laser treatment.

Fractional lasers strive to achieve the skin improvements obtained with ablative lasers (removal of skin, brown pigmentation, and wrinkles to promote collagen growth) without the associated side effects or downtime.

"When fractional resurfacing first appeared on the market, patients had more than a week of downtime where they would basically be in hiding. Patients said they wanted a procedure that would offer no such downtime," said Dr. Barry DiBernardo, a plastic surgeon in Montclair, New Jersey. "For the last few years, the latest fractional resurfacing machines offered a no-downtime option, but patients would need to have at least five sessions to see any improvement. More recently, machines have become available that offer visible results in one session with less than a week of social downtime."

"There are many different and new types of technology in fractional resurfacing," said Dr. Jason Pozner, a plastic surgeon from Boca Raton, Florida, discussing fractional resurfacing and comparing it with nonfractional resurfacing technologies. "With newer fractional technology, we can achieve very remarkable results with minimal to moderate downtime."

The newest laser treatments are done on an outpatient basis, with a recovery time between three and five days. Costs can range from several hundred to several thousand dollars, and because they are usually considered cosmetic, these procedures are generally not covered by insurance.

One device used is a new CO2-based fractional laser, DeepFX by Lumenis. "This device penetrates deeper than other devices we have used and is showing nice enhancement in wrinkles and acne scar patients," said Dr. Jeffrey Kenkel, a plastic surgeon in Dallas, Texas, who has been involved in the initial evaluation of the FDA-approved laser and will present his experience with the device as part of the FDA panel discussion.

Contour Lift, Feather Lift (APTOS Thread Lift)

There are several procedures that utilize threads similar to those used for stitches that are placed through the skin without cutting the skin and are used to lift the areas that suffer from sagging. The areas that can be treated are the cheeks, around the eyes, the brows, the jowls, and the neck. The procedure can provide quick and relatively bloodless lifting for patients who may need only little to moderate rejuvenation.

The threads have cogs, or barbs, which lie in one direction and open up; so when the threads are implanted into the subcutaneous fat and tugged into place, the tissue is then suspended and lifted. The threads are placed in carefully pre-determined areas of the face to support the tissue and lift it. The results improve over time as your own collagen surrounds the threads, causing the effect of further lifting.

This procedure is considered much less invasive than midface, face, and brow-lifts, requiring less operating room time (or none at all because it can be done in the office) and less downtime. There is often an immediate result; however, the results continue to improve over a three- to six-month period.

The Contour Lift technique allows for less slippage, longer-lasting results, and less visibility than other thread procedures. Some swelling and bruising can occur and usually goes away in 5 to 10 days. The downside to these procedures is the possibility that the threads lose their grip in the tissue, and the area lifted begins to sag again. There are individuals for whom the lift may not have taken effect at all.

Hair Removal

Permanent reduction in hair growth can be accomplished with electrolysis or lasers that destroy the hair follicles on any area of the body. The only area to avoid is the eyebrow area right above the eyelid itself. If a laser is used, the hair must be brown to black in order for the laser light to destroy the hair follicle.

Skin color and hair color are among factors a practitioner considers in determining the type of laser to use, duration of treatment, and number of treatments that may be necessary to accomplish desired results. Side effects of laser hair removal include post-treatment pain for a few minutes, skin redness for a few hours, and darkening of the skin for 2 to 12 months where the laser was applied. This darkening can be avoided by using bleaching cream a week before and a week after the treatment, along with sun avoidance.

Dermabrasion

Dermabrasion is a procedure in which a buffing device is used to sand down the skin to improve acne and chicken pox scarring, and to improve or remove wrinkles.

Surgical Cosmetic Procedures

The Lifestyle Lift

The Lifestyle Lift is a surgical procedure done with a local anesthetic in the office that lifts the loose skin jowls and neck, improves frown lines, wrinkles, and facial skin. With the Lifestyle Lift, excess fat is removed, the muscles are tightened, and the skin of the face and neck are lifted. Most people return to work or other normal activities in about a week. Results are immediate and natural-looking.

Mini Face-Lift

Younger patients may opt for a minimized lift known as a mini-face-lift, which lifts the areas of the neck, jowls, midface, or nasolabial folds. Endoscopic mini-face-lifts use tiny incisions behind the hairline and inside the mouth to lift muscle and skin tissue. Following the mini-face-lift, most people may return home the day of the procedure, and there is no lengthy recovery process.

Face-Lift

Full face-lift differs from the less invasive Lifestyle Lift and mini-face-lift. A full face-lift is usually combined with a neck and brow-lift. With a full face-lift, the deeper tissue is pulled up as well as the skin on top. (The less invasive procedures such as the Lifestyle Lift and mini-face-lift may only be a lift of the skin.) You may have more downtime and more out-of-pocket expense with the full face-lift; however, the results may be more significant and longer lasting than the Lifestyle Lift or mini-face-lift.

Liposuction and Tumescent Liposuction

Liposuction is great for sculpting the body, but it is not for weight loss. If you have fat deposits on your body that do not respond to diet or exercise, liposuction is a great option. Liposuction can also be used to improve saggy necks by giving a lifting and tightening effect. Liposuction can be done in the operating room under general anesthesia, or you can have the tumescent technique in which a numbing solution is painlessly injected into the fat to be removed. I recommend the tumescent technique because you do not have any risks associated with being put to sleep, and you can get up and leave the office immediately after the procedure.

What Is Safe for Skin of Color?

Topicals, Botox, all fillers, Thermage, light chemical peels such as glycolic acid or lactic acid, microdermabrasion, thread lifting procedures, liposuction, LipoLite (non-invasive body contouring similar to liposuction), and surgical procedures can be done. They will cause darkening of the skin, and can cause scarring called "keloids" to form if you are predisposed to them.

Part Six

ANTI-AGING FOR SKIN BY LOCATION AND COMPLAINT

What You Can Do About . . .

Recommendations Listed from Least Invasive to Most Invasive.

Lines around your mouth

Botox, Restylane, Juvederm, chemical peels, lasers such as Smooth-beam, Fraxel 2 the latest generation, Sciton, Erbium, CO_2 ultrapulse encore with active FX, plasma. Do not use straws or sport tops to drink out of and stop smoking.

Smile lines—the lines that run from the corners of your nose to your mouth

Fillers like Restylane, Juvederm, chemical peels, lasers such as Smoothbeam, Fraxel 2 the latest generation, Sciton, Erbium, CO_2 ulrapulse encore with active FX, feather lift, face-lift

Frown lines—the lines between your eyebrows

Botox, Restylane, Juvederm, chemical peels, lasers like Smooth-beam, Fraxel 2 the latest generation, Sciton, Erbium, CO_2 ultrpulse encore with active FX, surgical cutting of the muscles responsible for creating a frown

Lines under my eyes

Creams, lasers like Fraxel 2 the latest generation, Erbium, CO_2 ultrpulse encore with active FX, chemical peels

Crow's-feet—the lines on the lateral aspect of the eye

Botox, Restylane fine line, chemical peels, lasers such as Smooth-beam, Fraxel 2 the latest generation, Sciton, Erbium, CO_2 ultrpulse encore with active FX

Lines on your forehead

Botox is the best treatment for this issue. Restylane, Juvederm, chemical peels, lasers like Smoothbeam, Fraxel 2 the latest generation, Sciton, Erbium, CO_2 ultrapulse encore with active FX. A forehead-lift can help.

Lifting your forehead

Thermage, thread lifting procedure. Surgical brow-lift is used to reduce severe lines in the forehead and raise the eyebrows.

Lifting your eyebrows

Botox, Restylane, Juvederm Ultra, Thermage, thread lifting procedures, surgical brow-lift

Nasolabial folds—the lines from the corners of the nose to the corners of the mouth

Fillers, collagen, Captique, Hylaform, Restylane, Perlane, Juve-derm, Sculptra, Artefill, fat transfers, silicone, chemical peels, fotofacials, thread lifting procedures, lasers like Smoothbeam, Fraxel 2 the latest generation, Sciton, Erbium, CO_2 ultrapulse encore with active FX, face-lift

Lines on your cheeks

Fillers, collagen, Captique, Hylaform, Restylane, and Juvederm, chemical peels, fotofacials, thread lifting procedures, lasers like Smoothbeam, Fraxel 2 the latest generation, Sciton, Erbium, CO_2 ultrpulse encore with active FX, face-lift

Neck sagginess

Thermage, plasma, thread lifting procedures, liposuction, neck-lift, neck/lower face-lift

Lines on your neck

Botox, chemical peels, neck-lift, fotofacials, Sciton, plasma, lasers such as Fraxel 2 the latest generation, GentleYAG

Lines on your chest

ILPs, chemical peels, plasma, lasers such as Fraxel 2 the latest generation, Sciton, Erbium

Brown spots on your skin

Bleaching creams, liquid nitrogen, chemical peels, fotofacials, plasma, lasers such as Fraxel 2 the next generation, CO_2 Ultrapulse Encore with active FX, Alexandrite, and Erbium.

Aging hands, thin skin

Topicals, IPLs, liquid nitrogen, chemical peels, Restylane, fat transfers, plasma, lasers such as Sciton, Fraxel, GentleYAG

Wrinkles

Topicals, chemical peels, IPLs, plasma, lasers like Fraxel 2 the latest generation, Sciton, Erbium, GentleYAG

Saggy skin on your body

Ultrasound, Thermage, LipoLite, medical needling, surgical lifts

Spider veins

Sclerotherapy (injections into the veins; the most effective solution used for sclerotherapy is polidocanol foam), lasers like the Vbeam. Compression stockings should always be worn to prevent varicose veins if you sit or stand for long periods of time and during pregnancy.

Varicose veins

Sclerotherapy (injections into the veins). Large varicose veins can be removed by a small, heated probe or laser that is inserted into the varicose vein and is gently pulled through the length of the vein closing the vein as it goes. This works 95 percent of the time. Also, surgical stripping of the vessel. This procedure is called Endovenous Laser treatment.

Facial hair

Laser hair removal, electrolysis, removing the hair with any method that pulls the hair out by the root, then applying a topical called Vaniqa that blocks the growth of hair. Vaniqa reduces the amount of time between hair removal sessions, but it is only effective for as long as the cream is used.

Dark circles under your eyes

Control your allergies to food and airborne allergens. Topicals made for the eyes that have vita K, peptides, retinol, caffeine, sunscreen, light refractors.

Saggy skin under the eyes

Thermage, plasma, lasers like the Affirm, Sciton, Fraxel 2 the latest generation, Erbium, CO_2 ultrapulse encore with active FX, blehateroplasty (eyelid surgery) to correct "droopy" eyelids by removing excess pads and skin

Puffiness under the eyes

Topical eye gels that contain peptides and caffeine, cold black tea bags, surgical removal of the fat pad, control of allergies to food and various airborne particles

Large pores

Topical vitamin A preparations, (Retin-A, Retinol, Tazorac), AHAs (salicylic acid, glycolic acid, lactic acid), chemical peels, lasers

Blood vessels of the face

Lasers such as Iriderm, Vbeam Perfecta, GentleYAG, injections into the vessels called sclerotherapy, fotofacials, electrical desiccation (hot needle that cauterizes the vessels)

Unhealthy nails

Biotin. Do not use harsh chemicals, wash hands frequently, and avoid soaking in water. Collagen MD Type 1 & 3 by NeoCell Corp.

Short, thin eyelashes

Lumigan (also marketed as Latisse, available in a physician's office without a prescription) is used for glaucoma and can grow your eyelashes thick and long within six weeks. Nothing else on the market can compare. There are also eyelash growth products from Revitalash and John Marini.

Discomfort or pain of a procedure

Topical anesthetics, anti-anxiety medications like Valium, pain killers like Vicodin, Tylenol with codeine, nerve blocks, twilight sleep, and general anesthesia

About the Author

Bobbie Gee began her modeling career at 14. By 17, she was hired to teach makeup, fashion, and modeling at the largest self-improvement school in America.

In 1963, she became a fashion coordinator for one of Southern California's largest department store chains. A short time later, a Los Angeles TV executive hired her to produce and host two shows: *All about Women* and *Alone Together*.

After returning from the West Indies where her husband had accepted a two-year project, she accepted a public relations position at the Fashion Institute in Los Angeles. A few years later, she was contacted by the Walt Disney Company and, after surviving 16 interviews, was named Disneyland's Image Coordinator. After three years of problem solving for the company, she decided to follow a dream and goal she had set for herself at the age of 16 and became a professional speaker. Her career has taken her to 40 countries, and in 1993, she was inducted into the National Speakers Association Speaker Hall of Fame.

Bobbie is the author of the book *Creating a Million Dollar Image for Your Business*. She has been published by Nightingale-Conant, Simon & Schuster, PageMill Press, and Imagement, Seoul, South Korea.

For the past few years, she has taught life-enrichment classes for women on the nurturing of their physical, mental, emotional, and spiritual selves. The results include increased personal self-worth and confidence, leading the women to new heights.

Bobbie is the proud mother of two wonderful daughters and six grandchildren. She and her husband, Ernie, have been married 53 years. She is involved in church activities and loves to entertain and cook desserts.

Bobbie Gee Enterprises

Laguna Niguel, California

Bobbie Gee has designed presentations to benefit
your charity, church, or secular group. For information
on presentation dates available, please call:
(949) 661-5778

For information on how to order products mentioned in
Anti-Aging God's Way, please contact Bobbie at:
bobbiegee@earthlink.net

To reach Ms. Shien-Lin Garrett, PA-C, B.S., M.S.,
to address personal skin care problems or questions,
phone (949) 360-4400. Ms. Garrett is the assistant to:

Dr. Edward M. Kramer, M.D.
27995 Greenfield Drive, Suite C
Laguna Niguel, CA 92677

For more on Bobbie's speaking topics,
please visit her Web page:
www.bobbiegee.com